HOW TO GET A
RESEARCH DEGREE

A survival guide

Leonie Elphinstone
and
Robert Schweitzer

D1362873

ALLEN & UNWIN

First published in 1998
Allen & Unwin
9 Atchison Street, St Leonards 2065 Australia
Phone: (61 2) 9901 4088
Fax: (61 2) 9906 2218
E-mail: frontdesk@allen-unwin.com.au
Web: http://www.allen-unwin.com.au

National Library of Australia
Cataloguing-in-Publication entry:

How to get a research degree: a survival guide.

  Bibliography.
  Includes index.
  ISBN 1 86448 560 4.

  1. Graduate students. 2. Universities and colleges—
  Graduate work. 3. Study skills. I. Schweitzer, Robert,
  1950– . II. Elphinstone, Leonie. III. Title.

371.30281

Set in 11/13pt Adobe Garamond by Bookhouse Digital, Sydney
Printed by SRM Production Services Sdn Bhd, Malaysia

10 9 8 7 6 5 4 3 2 1

Foreword

Most postgraduate students come to understand, at some point during their years of study, that they had no idea what they were getting into, and had they known then what they know now, they would have selected a life path which pointed in the absolute opposite direction and headed down it at full speed. This realisation is born of the intermittent (in rare situations, unremitting) fear, insecurity, or sheer overwork that characterises the life of postgraduate scholarship. If you are such a student, in such a moment of awful realisation, you can now reach for your well-thumbed copy of Elphinstone and Schweitzer, and find here the advice, encouragement, and common sense that will help you through. Better yet, if you are just starting out or deciding to start out on a postgraduate path, this book will help prepare you for what lies ahead.

How To Get a Research Degree offers insight, instruction, and inspiration, and it does so without minimising the rigours of postgraduate study. It honours and normalises the many trials of the postgraduate research process, and in this it provides a great service to students. It brings to mind the observation of Professor Donald Fanger of Harvard University:

> Because the writer of a dissertation is almost always engaged in that activity for the first time, he or she is likely to believe that the awful problems which surface along the way are unique and unprecedented, and they must be signs of something gone alarmingly wrong ... [M]ost problems even (or especially) those that seem exclusively psychological are perfectly normal, common, standard. I have in mind depression, panic, tedium, and the sense of being locked into what Hegel called 'a bad infinity'.[1]

The aim of Elphinstone and Schweitzer is to guide you through the naturally rocky terrain of postgraduate study. They first provide you with an overview of the territory. Then they accompany you on the long journey through the research and writing process. They show you how to survive and thrive, where some of the dangers might lie and where the watering holes might be found. Should you fall into a Hegelian 'bad infinity', they throw out a line, point to some handholds to use in pulling yourself up. And they encourage you to pause occasionally in your progress, look back over the path so far, look deeply into yourself, and look forward into your post-postgraduate future, in order to fully understand the place of this trek in your longer life journey.

With the help of your teachers and mentors, and books like this one, you will come to understand postgraduate study as a process, not just a product, a process of asking and answering questions, and then asking and answering more questions. Many of these are at face value simple yes or no questions: 'Is my research problem clearly stated and defined?' 'Is my design adequate?' But these seemingly simple questions require many hours of reading, thought, writing and discussion to answer, and the answers may be complex or conditional rather than yes or no. Indeed, the asking and answering of questions is itself a learning process, at which you will get better with practice, just as you might get better at using a computer, negotiating with colleagues and supervisors, conducting statistical analyses, writing, or presenting your work in public.

When supervisors admonish you to 'Be organised' or 'Be proactive!' or 'Be concise in your writing!' the real task facing you is to become organised, to become proactive, to become precise to undergo a process, not just achieve an end state. The process of postgraduate study involves looking within yourself to assess your hopes, fears, goals, and your ongoing experience of learning. It involves looking outside of yourself, to engage with departmental policies, supervisors, peers, professionals in the field, literature, data, ideas. It involves your active interaction with the structures, materials, and people that constitute your learning environment.

Elphinstone and Schweitzer help students understand all this. They maintain a matter-of-fact attitude grounded in years of experience, numerous anecdotes and quotes, and reports of relevant research. Most importantly, they recognise each student as the lead explorer of his or her own unknown territory. They know that each student's self-reliance and sense of direction will be honed by the journey itself and will in turn determine the student's unique path and destination. I join them in wishing you well on your own journey, wherever it takes you.

Abigail Lipson, PhD
American University, Washington, DC, USA

---

[1] Donald Fanger. 1985, 'The Dissertation, From Conception to Delivery' in *On Teaching and Learning*, vol. 1. Harvard University Book Center for Teaching and Learning, pp. 26–33.

Contents

About the authors

LEONIE ELPHINSTONE is a psychologist with a Masters degree in higher education. Her Masters research involved the development of the first Australian version of the Course Experience Questionnaire. She has worked at three Australian universities as a counsellor and also as an educational consultant. She has previously produced a Manual for Postgraduate Supervisors at RMIT in Melbourne and a Bibliography of Selected References on Postgraduate Study. She has conducted workshops for both postgraduate supervisors and students and has researched the needs of postgraduate students.

DR ROBERT SCHWEITZER is Head of the Counselling Service at Queensland University of Technology. His own areas of postgraduate study have utilised a phenomenological methodology in the study of indigenous mental states and dream interpretation in a Xhosa-speaking community in South Africa. He has published numerous papers in areas of clinical psychology and supervised postgraduate theses to completion.

Acknowledgements

University life today is characterised by change, with emphasis on doing more with less resources and numerous debates about the direction of universities. Amid this change, however, there remains one core value—the pursuit of knowledge. Central to this endeavour is the research undertaken within the university, and many would argue that postgraduate students play a major role in this function.

For a number of years, we have run seminars for students and supervisors on getting the most out of supervision and effective supervisory practice. In conducting these seminars, we would like to personally acknowledge how much we have learned from the postgraduate students who have participated in our seminars, who agreed to be interviewed for the purposes of this book and have shared some of their success stories with a view to being helpful to others involved in research and postgraduate study.

The book covers a number of areas, some of which were outside our own areas of expertise. We would thus like to acknowledge the specialist input provided by David Mahony, Queensland University of Technology, who wrote chapters 8 and 9 covering the writing of a thesis, and Malcolm MacKenzie, University of Queensland, who wrote the final chapter entitled 'Careering into the future'. We are also grateful to Michael Lean, Queensland University of Technology, for his specialist advice on intellectual property rights.

We would like to thank Joyce Rawlins and Geoff Foster for their assistance in the typing and editing of the text respectively; Associate Professor David Hawke, Queensland University of Technology, for the drawings; and Yoni Ryan, Queensland University of Technology, for allowing us to reproduce the Role Perception Scale which is incorporated in this book.

Finally, it has been our pleasure to work with the highly competent and professional staff at Allen & Unwin.

Leonie Elphinstone and Robert Schweitzer

Introduction

Working in universities we have become increasingly aware that postgraduate study makes particular demands on both students and supervisors to meet the traditional challenges of scholarship in a rigorous, effective and efficient manner. Our aims in writing this book are to outline how a postgraduate student can make effective choices at the beginning of the process of postgraduate study which will increase the chances of completion, to provide some strategies to avoid and/or overcome some of the hurdles which may arise during the course of postgraduate study and to value the interpersonal dimensions of postgraduate study. We trust that this book will be useful to students who may be contemplating postgraduate study,, students who are already engaged in the process of postgraduate study or academics actively involved in the supervision of postgraduate study.

In writing this book we have sought the experience of postgraduate students directly involved in research with a view to examining the components of their experience which contributed to success. We have taken the view that postgraduate study is not only a technical exercise but also one which involves positive relationships with supervisors, fellow students, and potential and future colleagues.

Our approach

The thesis is the end product of a process, and equal importance should be attached to managing that process as well as maintaining a focus on the end product. We believe that postgraduate students need to be proactive from the beginning, actively managing the process for ultimate success.

Organisation of the text

How to Get a Research Degree is divided into thirteen chapters. The first seven chapters focus on life as a postgraduate researcher. The next five chapters deal with the technical aspects of the thesis. The final chapter looks specifically at postgraduate study and careers. The text is enlivened by the contributions of postgraduate students who, of course, have first-hand experience in constructing a thesis.

Note that there is some terminology that differs between Australia, the United Kingdom and the United States. In the United States 'a supervisor' is referred to as 'an advisor'. Also postgraduate study in Australia and the United Kingdom is equivalent to graduate study in the United States.

chapter 1

Getting started

When I decided to enrol for a Masters by research, I thought I'd approach a supervisor I knew well to supervise me. I knew his area of interest and I was fairly flexible about what I worked on, so I asked him if he had a viable project which I could assist with. I ended up in a team with three other students, all working on different parts of the project. After five months it became clear that I needed to consider doing a PhD. I had a project related to my work which I wanted to research. I ended up with an industry-based associate supervisor while my primary supervisor was an academic. They had very different styles and knowledge but in combination they were able to give me what I needed, although at times I had to be very assertive and clear regarding what I thought the project was about.

—Martin, a PhD student in Engineering

Postgraduate study provides an exciting opportunity to make a significant contribution to knowledge, to choose a topic in which you have a deep or passionate interest, and to engage in academic debate with a supervisor who offers you the opportunity to participate fully in a community of scholars.

This interaction with others in the academic community is central to the whole postgraduate process and to your personal development as a scholar. Although you will be working independently in the development of your topic and in the ensuing research, in many ways your networking with others will allow you to develop insights and perspectives outside your own mindset. Therefore, the development of your research area is closely related to your early interactions with your academic department.

For many students, finding a supervisor will be closely intertwined with selecting and developing a thesis topic. In most cases, students will have a topic area in mind when approaching supervisors. However, this varies according to the discipline in which you are enrolling. It is important to remember that both effective supervision and the development of an appropriate research topic are critical to success in postgraduate study. Even in a situation where a supervisor proposes a thesis topic and invites you to work with them, you need to be sure that the topic and type of supervision being offered are appropriate for you. Be proactive and selective in your choice of topic and supervisor. After all, two to five years or more is a long time to try to persist with inappropriate choices.

This chapter focusses on defining what a thesis should be, and how to develop a viable thesis topic that will enable you to approach potential supervisors and, possibly, sources for funding. The following chapter focusses on finding an appropriate supervisor, clarifying initial expectations and managing the relationship effectively.

WHAT IS A THESIS?

The word 'thesis', derived from the Greek term *tithenai*, refers to 'a position or that which is set down or advanced for argument: a subject for scholastic exercise: an essay on a theme'.

To write a thesis is, traditionally, to present an argument, and it will usually have four clearly identifiable parts:

- *Proposition.* A statement or a set of statements which you are about to defend and prove.
- *Justification.* Identifying the purpose and value of your work, and surveying the existing literature to show how

your work fits into the broad framework of knowledge and theory in the area.

- *Evidence.* Evidence to support your position may be derived from authorities in the field, from experimental results and interviews, and by using statistics and deductions drawn from analogy and logic. This is the body of your thesis.
- *Proof.* This will be your conclusion, and will also involve a summary of the important points you have raised.

Many students initially enrol in a Masters degree by research anticipating that they may be able to convert to a Doctor of Philosophy (PhD) program at the end of a couple of years. If you commence your research with this idea, you should be clear about what the policy of the faculty or school is; for instance, whether or not they allow this sort of transition and under what conditions. It is also important to be clear about the distinctions between a Masters degree and a PhD. This information can also assist you to set some boundaries on your research, particularly if you are undertaking a Masters rather than a PhD.

DISTINCTION BETWEEN A MASTERS AND A DOCTORAL DEGREE

There are accepted differences between a doctoral program and a Masters degree by research. Generally, a PhD has greater breadth, depth and intention than a Masters degree, as indicated by the following lists of criteria (Madsen, 1983):

Masters degree by research

1. Evidence of an original investigation or the testing of ideas.
2. Competence in independent work or experimentation.
3. An understanding of appropriate techniques.
4. Ability to make critical use of published work and source materials.

5. Appreciation of the relationship of the special theme to the wider field of knowledge.
6. Contains material worthy of publication.

Doctoral degree

Points 1–6 above, plus:

7. Originality, as shown by the topic researched or the methodology employed.
8. Distinct contribution to knowledge.

Universities may have their own written policy on the distinction between doctoral and Masters by research programs, so it is vital to read all policy descriptions provided. Your supervisor, if experienced in supervising both PhDs and Masters projects, may also be able to provide you with a clear working distinction. If there are copies of Masters and PhD theses held in your department or library, it is also useful to compare those which deal with similar or related topics.

CHOOSING A THESIS TOPIC

There are at least two schools of thought on choosing a topic. The conventional approach is that you are responsible for choosing a topic and then finding an appropriate person to supervise the topic. The alternative approach is to choose the supervisor first; for instance, someone with whom you think you can work well. You might then decide to undertake a study in the selected supervisor's area of expertise.

If you are choosing your own topic area, rather than being assigned an area by your supervisor, remember that the topic must be able to sustain your interest and enthusiasm for several years, depending on your enrolment. For some students, choosing a topic which is 'too close to home', or too personally relevant, may be a mistake in terms of objectivity. Trying to find the perfect topic may also be a mistake; after all, your topic will change as you gradually refine it and redefine boundaries, directions and limitations.

Most students will need initially to spend large amounts of time in the university library, working through journals and past theses in the relevant area, getting a feel for what has been done and what might be possible. When you are looking for potential topics you need to be aware of the various paradigms which guide research and the implications of these paradigms for the types of research which are possible. These can be classified into three basic types:

1. Basic research, which involves exploring a new problem or issues about which little is known.
2. Strategic research, which involves testing out the limits of previous research findings.
3. Applied research, which usually begins with a real world problem which has to be defined and then a solution developed.

The first and last of these are where enthusiastic new post-graduate students often start, having an ideal topic in mind with seemingly large potential for innovative research. However, the problem with these two types of research is that uncharted territory is difficult to define and boundaries are hard to set. Both of these types of research rely heavily on the expertise of the supervisor in terms of definition and limit setting. Whereas strategic research, by its nature, is defined from the beginning, often with a clearly defined methodology. This type of research may initially seem a less exciting option; however, it may be less troublesome and provide greater chance of success.

Many research students discover that, for a variety of reasons, through the process of topic definition they are led down or have chosen to follow different paths to those they anticipated at the beginning. It's important to be flexible as time progresses, accepting changes in direction, hurdles and other problems as part of the course of the research. These may lead to an equally successful, although unanticipated, outcome.

Charles Handy (1989) describes this learning process as a cycle or wheel which involves enquiry, action and reflection. An adaption of the process is shown in Figure 1.1. The representation of learning as a wheel is particularly apt when it comes to postgraduate research. It emphasises the process of going round and round as you refine the questions to be asked and review the literature, develop methodologies and evaluate or test your ideas, and continually reflect on the process. This process may be applied to objective approaches as well as to qualitative perspectives on research.

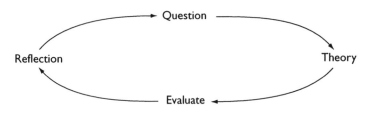

Figure 1.1 The research cycle

DEFINING YOUR THESIS TOPIC

When you have a broad thesis area in mind, there are some questions you will need to ask yourself in order to clarify and define your thesis topic:

- Is there an appropriate supervisor available?
- Has the topic already been overworked?
- Is the project substantial enough for a thesis?
- Is the problem clearly stated and defined?
- Is the problem researchable?
- Could the resolution of the problem make an important or significant contribution to knowledge or practice?
- Is the scope of the research appropriate for the degree?
- Are there limitations inherent in the research project stated?
- Is the terminology adequate?
- Are assumptions clearly stated?

- Are there appropriate resources available to carry out the project?
- Are there areas of the project which would require you to develop new skills? If so, how would you go about this?
- Would the research findings be useful to the participants or others in some way?

Most departments will require an outline of your topic area at an early stage of your program. If you are seeking a supervisor in the department, then this may be a critical part of your approach. You will need to know the expertise of staff members in the department and be prepared to adapt your topic to fit within those realms of expertise. Alternatively, if you are being assigned a topic by your supervisor or are working as part of a research team on a larger project, you will work with your supervisor to define a thesis outline to submit to the department or faculty for acceptance.

The type of outline required will depend on the faculty in which you are working and the guidelines provided. Disciplines differ greatly in the type of information necessary for an outline and a thesis proposal. Guidelines published by your department will be useful, but reading successful outlines submitted by previous students in your faculty or department may be a more helpful guide to what is acceptable. The department may keep copies of thesis proposals on file or your own supervisor may be able to provide some. Unsuccessful proposals can also be useful in indicating potential problems and pitfalls.

METHODOLOGY AND RESEARCH DESIGN

The broad range of disciplines which now offer postgraduate study by research is matched by an ever-increasing range of possible methodologies and approaches to postgraduate research. The appropriateness and effectiveness of any chosen methodology will be largely determined by the problem being considered and the assumptions we hold about the world. Postgraduate research is obviously about knowledge and the pursuit of knowledge, and there are many ways in which we are able to gain knowledge. The traditional scientific approach has been valued in many areas: it is based specifically upon particular methodologies and relies upon gathering data and/or measurement. Some characteristics of this approach include experimentation, measurement, analysis, determined reactions, an independent observer and quantifiable observations.

Fortunately, there are now many other alternative methodologies which are based upon qualitative or verbal descriptions and which emphasise the meanings of phenomena. In this case, the essential question then becomes not how do we measure phenomena, but rather what do the phenomena mean? This approach to knowledge relies on meaning, explication, intentional responses, a recognition that central phenomena are only known through various manifestations and participant observation. No doubt there are other approaches and other paradigms for bringing about knowledge.

Research, therefore, may be empirically based; that is, deduced from sensory experience, observation and measurement and/or qualitatively based, being more concerned with meaning and the explication of meaning. The research question which you are considering, as well as your assumptions about the world, will be the main defining factors in the determination of the methodology chosen, along with the discipline area. The issue of methodology and design cannot therefore be considered in isolation, but only within the context of the research question to be investigated.

Once you have established your area of interest, you need then to consider the appropriate types of methodology. As indicated earlier, if you are undertaking strategic research which seeks to test out the findings of previous research and the generalisations implied in that research, then the methodology to be used will most likely be clearly indicated. However, if you are undertaking basic or applied research which is attempting to look at a new problem, then the methodology you employ will be determined by the type of problem and possibly the boundaries set by the discipline in which you are undertaking research.

Clearly you need to interact with your potential supervisor to decide on your methodology and design. At this stage it is vital for you to determine if your supervisor has the expertise to supervise you in the methodology chosen or, alternatively, to ensure that you are able to consult other experts in the methodology area, within or outside your faculty. Ultimately, you need to be sure that the methodology suits the problem and that your supervisor or other adviser is conversant with the methodology and the theoretical underpinnings of the methodology. When it comes to assessment you will need to be confident that the methodology is likely to be acceptable to potential assessors.

THE RESEARCH PROPOSAL

In many cases, students start with a brief proposal which is progressively refined over a period of six to twelve months. This process varies from faculty to faculty, but generally a well-structured proposal will facilitate your progress. Whether you are looking for a suitable supervisor or seeking funding from another educational institution, government body or private enterprise, it is important to put together a well-designed and coherent research proposal to improve your chances of acceptance and success. If you are a novice, this will be a welcome challenge.

Suggested components for the research proposal are:

- topic
- rationale, including a brief review of relevant literature (a draft of the literature review should be included as an appendix)
- aims and objectives
- design (if appropriate, instruments should be included as an appendix)
- outcomes expected
- structure of the proposed thesis, in summary

- proposed time frame for the research
- supervisor's name
- date
- references.

CRITERIA FOR ASSESSING A RESEARCH PROPOSAL

The following criteria are commonly used by departments or faculties for assessing research proposals:

- clearly defined research aims and objectives
- feasibility of research project
- appropriate project size or scope for level of study (e.g. Masters or PhD)
- appropriate research design
- evidence that the research approach will achieve its objectives
- familiarity with literature in the field and with the chosen research methodology
- evidence of scholarly writing
- relevance.

What postgraduate students say

What advice would you have for a potential postgraduate student about their first thesis proposal?

- Plenty of consultation is needed with your supervisor.
- Get feedback from other students and peers who work in the field.
- Take time to get to know the research area really well before you write about it.
- Be clear about what it is you aim to do.
- Master your computer.
- Look at other students' proposals.
- Browse through your supervisor's thesis.

CHECKLIST OF QUESTIONS TO BE ASKED ABOUT A RESEARCH PROPOSAL

In preparing your research proposal, or once you have written your proposal, you may ask yourself the following questions. Some of the questions relating to research design may be less relevant for a qualitative study. If you are able to answer the majority of the questions in the affirmative you are well on the way to success.

The research question

The question

What is your research problem/question?

- Is the problem clearly stated?
- Is the question focussed enough to enable you to state specific hypotheses and test them?
- Is there enough substantial information for you to gain sufficient data?

The hypotheses

What are your hypotheses?

- Have you considered the practical aspects of designing ways of testing these hypotheses?

The objectives

What are your underlying objectives?

- Are these appropriate for this research proposal?

Background to the question

Significance and relevance

What is the significance and relevance of your proposed research?

- How does your proposed research tie in with current theory?
- What are the implications for application?
- What would be possible applications of the information/knowledge gained from your research?
- Does the proposed research have the potential to contribute to knowledge?

Literature review

Have you surveyed the relevant literature adequately?

- Is your research adequately related to other people's work on the same or similar topics?
- What weaknesses or gaps are evident in the current literature?
- Does your proposal address these gaps or weaknesses, or build on strategies in the current knowledge of this area?

Research design

Definitions

Have you clearly defined all concepts and variables (theoretically and operationally)?

Design

Is your design adequate?

- Does your design meet formal standards for consistency?
- Is your design appropriate to the problem and objectives?
- In some areas you will need to ask yourself whether negative results be meaningful?
- Have you controlled possible misleading and confounding variables?
- How are the independent and dependent variables measured or specified?

Techniques

What instruments or techniques will you use to gather data?

- Are the reliabilities and validities of these techniques well established?

Participants

- Is the population (to which generalisations are to be aimed) clearly specified?
- Is there a specific and acceptable method of drawing a sample from this population?

Setting

What is the setting in which you will gather data?

- Is it feasible and practical to carry out the research plan in this setting?
- Is the cooperation of the necessary persons obtainable?
- Is relevant equipment available to support your study?
- Is relevant expertise available to support your study?

Analysis

How are the data to be analysed?

- What techniques of 'data reduction' have you considered?
- Are methods specified for analysing data qualitatively?
- Are methods specified for analysing data quantitatively?

Resources

Resources

In light of available resources, how feasible is your design?

- What compromises will you need to make in translating an idealised research design into a practical research design?
- What limitations or generalisations will result?

- What will be needed in terms of time, money, personnel and facilities?
- Are these available for this proposal?

Time frame

Have you broken down the research plan into a series of sequential steps with a realistic time frame specified for each?

As a general rule of thumb, allocate approximately one-sixth of the time allocated to your research for final 'writing up' and submission of the research thesis. A recent graduate in engineering suggested that the actual time required to write up a thesis is pi multiplied by the time you thought it would take, or in mathematical terms:

$$t_{real} = \pi \ t_{imagined}$$

Ethics

Does your proposal meet relevant ethical guidelines?

- Have ethical issues associated with this research been considered?
- Will you require approval from an Ethics Committee?
- Is the research relevant?

Finally, it is considered courteous to tell people who have participated in your research about the outcomes and to thank them for their participation.

chapter 2

Choosing a supervisor

As a mature age student, I looked for a supervisor who was approachable and easy to talk to. Unfortunately, I grabbed the first one I could find who was interested in my topic area without looking at his research background, publications and reputation as a supervisor. It turned out that he knew nothing about the area, and after six months I took a leave of absence feeling very disillusioned with the whole process. It was partly my lack of understanding about what a research thesis would involve and partly the lack of adequate supervision.

Two years later I returned, much clearer about what I wanted. I sought a supervisor with a good track record of research, plenty of publications and a reasonable personal style. It worked well because she was very interested in my topic, had the appropriate background knowledge and understood the scope of a Masters project. She also had a lot of influence in the department which helped me to get the resources I needed.

—Rab, a Masters graduate in Sociology

Having a supervisor who was not just academically very good but also very approachable, easygoing and personable really made a big difference. Rather than being detached, unavailable and difficult to communicate with, my supervisor was a very welcoming person who made me feel at ease. As a graduate student I don't think you have the confidence you attain a few years further down the track, so a supervisor needs to be a responsible and sympathetic person.

—Marianne, a PhD student in International Politics

Selecting a good supervisor with whom you can work in a productive way is critical to your success as a postgraduate student. Even if a supervisor selects you to work with them, you need to be sure that the supervisory relationship will work for you. It is impossible to overstate the importance of this relationship to your success in the research process.

Effective supervisors are most likely to have some of the following characteristics:

- a personal interest in your topic area
- a good reputation as an academic
- a good reputation as a supervisor
- positive personality characteristics (such as warmth and friendliness)
- a track record of successful candidates.

What postgraduate students say

What are the qualities you look for in an effective supervisor?

- someone with a genuine interest in the topic and in supervising you
- someone with outstanding research experience
- someone with empathy for students and all the demands placed on them
- someone who is approachable and easy to talk to
- someone who has a good background in your research area
- someone you can feel comfortable with
- someone who is easy to get along with
- someone who is accessible.

You will need to be clear and assertive about your needs and be able to negotiate effectively with your supervisor on the roles you each take in the process. You may need to make a choice between someone who is fully conversant with your chosen area—a technical expert—and someone with whom you can interact well on a personal level. It will be a rare supervisor who can provide everything that you are seeking. You may also need to utilise other resources and individuals with specialisations in areas outside your supervisor's range of expertise. As a postgraduate student you have to be a good networker, prepared to initiate contact with experts both in your field and out of it.

Supervisors also have certain expectations of the behaviour and performance of the postgraduate students they supervise. As a minimum, they normally expect candidates to be:

- independent, self-motivated and able to show initiative
- able to write in clear, legible English
- open to advice, comments and criticism from others
- prepared to follow up the advice they are given
- ready for regular meetings
- able to report honestly about their progress.

(Phillips and Pugh, 1994)

Supervisors will normally expect to learn from their postgraduate students as the students progressively become expert in the thesis area. They may also expect to develop a collegial relationship in the long run, eventually sharing publications and research, depending on the discipline in which the research is done.

What supervisors say

What are the qualities you look for in a postgraduate student?

- I like students with a lot of initiative. It's the way I operate I guess … I often don't know myself exactly what sort of project we're going into and how it is going to end up.
- I think good supervision is when you have a close relationship—a close professional relationship with your student in that they can come and talk to you a lot, they sound out a lot of ideas as they're going along and they do things in a way which enables you to help them as much as possible.

(Adapted from Cullen et al. 1994, pp. 50–65)

PROBLEMS IN THE SUPERVISORY RELATIONSHIP

When you are making arrangements for supervision, it is helpful to be aware of the common difficulties that arise so you can avoid some of the pitfalls. You should bear in mind that personality, professional and organisational factors can determine the quality of the student–supervisor relationship.

When talking about supervision, postgraduate students often complain of the following (Moses, 1992):

Personality factors

- neglect by supervisor
- clash of personalities
- barriers to communication arising from age, cultural and language differences
- personal differences in approach to work.

Professional factors

- supervisors who are misinformed or supervisors without sufficient knowledge in the area supervised
- supervisors with few genuine research interests or research interests which are different from those of the student.

Organisational factors

- supervisors having too many students to supervise
- supervisors too busy with administration
- supervisors unable to manage the research group effectively
- departmental or school arrangements and facilities which isolate the student
- inadequate support services and equipment not available.

What postgraduate students say

What pitfalls should be avoided when selecting a supervisor?

- Don't take the first one 'offered'—shop around.
- Avoid supervisors with different or incompatible research areas.
- Avoid those with whom you feel you cannot communicate easily.
- Avoid supervisors with little or no previous experience in supervising students, little time to see students and lack of knowledge of the standards of thesis required.

Don't take the first supervisor offered—shop around.

Supervisors and students are subject to the same biases, personal attractions and issues of power as everyone else in the community. Ignoring this may lead to difficulties, miscommunication and overall dysfunction of the relationship. If such issues arise, it is advisable to talk through them rather than 'act out' these feelings in a potentially destructive or self-defeating manner. If you are not sure how to approach the matter, discuss it with a counsellor at your university.

Supervisors are rarely independent of influences within their environment, hence you need to look carefully at the total context in which you will be supervised, including organisational factors in the department and the faculty and the nature of the discipline in which you are studying.

CHOOSING A FACULTY OR DEPARTMENT

Many students focus on obtaining a suitable supervisor regardless of the department or faculty in which they are located. In some cases, students will be very familiar with the department, having completed their undergraduate degree with the same academic staff. Even if you know the department, it is important to ask about facilities and resources for postgraduates. In many departments there is a noticeable difference in the treatment of undergraduates and postgraduates, with the latter being considered part of the overall academic culture of the department. The faculty or department policy and attitude towards postgraduates, and the provision of resources for them, can have a significant effect on postgraduates enrolled in that area.

When you approach a faculty, department or school to enquire about enrolment and supervision for postgraduate study, you should ask about the following resources and practices:

- Is there a postgraduate student handbook for the department or faculty, or only a general one for the whole university?
- Is there a departmental or faculty-based document which describes good supervisory practice?

- Do the staff seem concerned with carefully matching supervisors and prospective students?
- Are regular meetings between students and supervisors encouraged?
- Does there seem to be an ethos of supporting and promoting postgraduate study?
- Are there regular meetings between academic staff and postgraduates (e.g. in an academic forum)?
- Are there specific resources available for postgraduate students (e.g. computers, rooms, etc.)?
- Do postgraduates have access to the Internet and e-mail, including dial-in access? What charges, if any, are involved?
- Is there a postgraduate coordinator who deals with supervision and other issues and has time allotted specially for this task?
- Is there a postgraduate students' association or a regular meeting time and place for postgraduate students in the department or faculty?

The answers to these questions may indicate something about the attitude towards postgraduate students and their significance in the overall academic culture of the department.

DISCIPLINE-BASED DIFFERENCES IN SUPERVISION STYLES

The faculty in which you are enrolling, and thus the discipline base, will significantly affect the style of supervision that you will experience. For instance, if you are in a laboratory-based or more technically based discipline, you may see your supervisor daily while working and thus have fewer formal meetings with them. If you are working in a humanities or arts-based area, you may rarely see your supervisor unless you make a specific time, and you may spend large amounts of time working alone away from the university. Table 2.1 shows some of the other patterns associated with these differences (Whittle, 1992).

Table 2.1 Comparison of supervision in Arts and Science

	Arts	Science
Supervision style	'Hands off'	Close, mentoring
Meetings	Irregular, infrequent	Regular, frequent
Joint publication	Uncommon	The norm
Mentorship	Rare	The norm

Other disciplines will also vary greatly in the style of supervision expected. If you are not already clear about the style in your discipline, ask other postgraduates in your area.

Overall, remember that you can be active in choosing a supervisor and ask pertinent questions early in the process to avoid some of the pitfalls later. Remember also to look at the whole context—the department, faculty and discipline—and to consider the style of supervision you personally need and that which is on offer to you.

Exercise

The Role Perception Scale (see below) will assist you to clarify your expectations of supervisors. You can complete it alone initially and ask potential supervisors to indicate what their view is on some or all of the issues. It is a useful starting point for finding out if you have compatible attitudes to some major supervision issues.

THE ROLE PERCEPTION SCALE

Read each pair of statements listed below. Each expresses a standpoint that supervisors and students may take. You may not agree fully with either of the statements; in this case, estimate your position and mark it on the scale. For example, if you believe very strongly that supervisors should select the research topic, you would circle '1' on scale 1.

Topic/course of study

1	It is a supervisor's responsibility to select a promising topic	1 2 3 4 5 It is a student's responsibility to select a promising topic
2	In the end, it is up to the supervisor to decide which theoretical frame of reference is most appropriate	1 2 3 4 5 A student has the right to choose a theoretical standpoint even if it conflicts with that of the supervisor
3	A supervisor should direct a student in the development of an appropriate program of research and study	1 2 3 4 5 A student should be able to work out a schedule and research program appropriate to their needs
4	A supervisor should ensure that a student has access to all necessary facilities	1 2 3 4 5 Ultimately, the student must find the necessary facilities to complete their research

Contact/involvement

5	Supervisor–student relationships are purely professional and personal relationships should not develop	1 2 3 4 5 Close personal relationships are essential for successful supervision
6	A supervisor should initiate frequent meetings with a student	1 2 3 4 5 A student should initiate meetings with their supervisor
7	A supervisor should check constantly that a student is on track and working consistently	1 2 3 4 5 Students should have the opportunity to find their own way without having to account for how they spend their time
8	A supervisor should terminate the candidature if they think a student will not succeed	1 2 3 4 5 A supervisor should support the student regardless of their opinion of the student's capability

The thesis

9 A supervisor should ensure that the thesis is finished not much later than the minimum period	1 2 3 4 5	As long as a student works steadily they can take as long as they need to finish the work
10 A supervisor has direct responsibility for the methodology and content of the thesis	1 2 3 4 5	A student has total responsibility for ensuring that the methodology and content of the thesis are appropriate to the discipline
11 A supervisor should assist in the actual writing of the thesis if the student has difficulties, and should ensure that the presentation is flawless	1 2 3 4 5	A student must take full responsibility for presentation of the thesis, including grammar and spelling
12 A supervisor should insist on seeing drafts of every section of the thesis in order to review them in a timely fashion	1 2 3 4 5	It is up to a student to ask for constructive criticism from a supervisor

(Ryan and Whittle, 1996, adapted from Moses, 1985)

chapter 3

Managing your relationship with your supervisor

My supervisor would always insist that I visit her at home for supervision. While she read my drafts, she asked that I do her ironing. I thought that was the normal way of supervision until I went to a second supervisor who behaved quite differently.

—Beatrice, a PhD student in Genetics

I think that a student has to know what they want from a supervisor in the first place. You have to be able to say 'I need you to look at this piece of work and I need you to look at it within the next two weeks.' Everybody has loads to do in their lives so you can't sit back and wait; you have to be someone who pushes a bit to get through it, so I think that has to be part of your role.

—Deborah, a PhD student in English Literature

At first it is difficult to know what you should and can expect from supervisors. The potential power relationship which exists between supervisors and students can further cloud the issue. Fortunately, more and more information exists within university faculties and departments outlining supervisory responsibilities and expectations. In this chapter we will be outlining strategies and approaches you can use to optimise your management of the supervisory situation in order to maximise the assistance you receive.

The relationship with your supervisor is one of the most important factors in gaining your postgraduate award. Over the period of a research thesis you will need to interact frequently with your supervisor. There is no doubt that both of you will experience periods of frustration; the relationship is likely to be intense. As the research enterprise is important to you, it is likely that you will feel elation, doubt, anger, admiration and a variety of other emotions which are a common part of this type of interaction. It is vital that a sense of trust develops between you and your supervisor and that, overall, the relationship is experienced as an affirming one.

The first couple of meetings should focus on how the supervision process is going to work between you. Have your supervisor specify the roles they expect to take, the frequency of meetings and the ways in which potential difficulties may be resolved. You will need to ask a number of relevant questions at the beginning to ensure that your expectations are realistic and are compatible with those of your supervisor.

You need to exchange information with your supervisor about other aspects of your work and personal life so that you both have a clear picture of where the supervisory relationship fits. Get to know what other commitments or research projects your supervisor is involved in. This will give you a clear picture of how your research and supervision fits into their total role. Give your supervisor information about your own commitments, which should be possible once you have completed the role diagram outlined in chapter 4. It is useful for them to understand the relationship between the thesis, the other roles you fulfil and your future goals. The Role Perception Scale in chapter 2 provides a useful way for you to clarify your perceptions and expectations.

What supervisors say

- One of the things I say at the beginning is: 'How often we see each other is up to you and to me.' We sit and talk about what our expectations are and what we'd like.
- I warn that I will be making the running in the first few weeks and insist on seeing them fairly frequently. After that, as far as I'm concerned, the frequency can drop off to once a month. However, if they want to increase the frequency that's up to them.
- When I am not reading material, I'm just talking to them about their progress. Either way there will often be some administrative things to sort out. If there is field work there will be administrative issues, so a monthly meeting is useful.

(Adapted from Cullen et al., 1994, pp. 50–65)

BEING PROACTIVE: ISSUES TO DISCUSS WITH YOUR SUPERVISOR

It is generally recognised that students will need their supervisor more than their supervisor will need them, and therefore it is important to be proactive in managing the relationship. Before a meeting with your supervisor it is helpful to draft an agenda which includes the items you want to discuss. The following issues should be clarified early on with your supervisor, and some may need to be renegotiated during the research process:

1. What is a thesis?

- What does 'thesis' mean?
- What is the appropriate structure?
- What is the appropriate length?
- What referencing conventions should be used?
- What is the difference between a thesis that passes and one that is first class?

- What are the titles of good examples of theses in this field?
- What is meant by 'originality'?
- Who owns papers arising during and after thesis supervision?

2. Meetings

- What should the frequency and duration of meetings be?
- What will be the structure of meetings, e.g. is there a need for written reports to be discussed?
- What is the access to supervisor outside of scheduled meeting times?
- Who has the responsibility to initiate meetings (if not scheduled regularly)?
- What is the protocol when one person can't make the meeting?

3. Advice and support

- Development of the research proposal: how much input will there be from the supervisor, and how will this proceed?
- Expectations of feedback: how much, how often, in what form, with how much notice?
- Support with theoretical content, e.g. resources, contacts. How much can be expected given the supervisor's knowledge of the area?
- Support in methodology training—will the supervisor assist, or organise other support?
- What methods and standards of record-keeping does the supervisor expect or recommend?
- What other kinds of knowledge are needed in support of the research process, such as academic writing.
- What resources does the supervisor know of, and how much help can they give?
- When should thesis sections be given to the supervisor; when should the work be returned with critical comment?
- Will the supervisor also comment on drafts of research papers?
- Are there relevant personal circumstances that might make the supervision or completion of the thesis difficult, e.g. the

student suffering financial hardship or other personal difficulties, or the supervisor going on study or any other leave?

4. Time frame

- How long should the different stages take to complete?
- What would be a realistic completion date in view of student and supervisor's separate commitments and faculty/university policy?

5. Joint supervisors

- What roles will be taken by principal and associate supervisors, e.g. different theoretical and training inputs?
- If there is a disagreement about methods between joint supervisors, how will it be resolved?

6. Student expectations of resources

- What faculty handbooks or other documents are relevant?
- Are there regular faculty forums which postgraduate students can attend or participate in?

Do you have access to the following:

- study place (desk, chair, bookshelf, filing cabinet, phone, mailbox)?
- personal computer and printer?
- tea/coffee facilities?
- photocopying, stationery, etc.?
- paid work, such as tutoring?
- funding for research, travel or conference grants?
- support services, e.g. technical, secretarial?
- Internet, e-mail, facsimile, telephone, etc.?
- technical assistance if appropriate?

7. Faculty/research centre expectations of the student

- Seminar presentation of the thesis in progress?
- Coursework?
- Conference attendance/presentation?

- Oral examination?

8. What university/faculty documents are available on supervision?

9. Resolving problems with supervision

- What are the faculty procedures for monitoring the supervision in the event that one of the parties is not happy with its progress?
- What university protocols are available in the event that one of the parties is not happy with the progress of supervision and the difficulties cannot be resolved within the faculty?

10. Clarification of program assessment

- How is the coursework assessed?
- How is the thesis proposal and the first year's progress assessed?
- How is the assessment of the thesis conducted?
- What happens afterwards?
- How are examiners chosen?
- What are the protocols for extensions and deferment?

11. Ethics

- What ethical issues need to be considered in the research project?
- Do you need to apply for consent from an appropriate university committee?
- Is there an independent ethics adviser available to you as a student?

12. Intellectual and industrial property

- Are there aspects of your research which make a formal agreement necessary or desirable?
- If so, how do you go about this?

It is entirely appropriate for you to ask your supervisor for a copy of theses which they have successfully supervised. If this is their first experience of supervising a thesis, you may find the supervisor's own thesis of interest in enabling you to better understand the requirements for the task ahead.

What supervisors say

- The hardest thing for me is to know how much to leave to the student and how much to do myself after a year or two years.
- They have lots of help to begin with and then, like a teenager, they want to do their own thing. And, like a teenager, they're not always able to.
- You can help a student too much and then they may be a bit frustrated that they haven't had the chance to really do their own thing.

(Adapted from Cullen et al., 1994, pp. 50–65)

GENERAL COMMENTS

Meet regularly, relate honestly with your supervisor and develop an awareness of their style, expertise and interests.

If you have problems with your project, raise them early rather than allowing resentment to build up. Confront problems in the supervisory relationship as they arise. If you are unhappy with this relationship and can't sort it out directly with your supervisor, find out who deals with such disputes in your school or department. Discuss the issue with them in order to find a solution which will allow you to continue successfully.

If your university has a postgraduate students' association, then they may have an adviser who can assist you. Alternatively, try the Counselling Service.

chapter 4

Keeping your life balanced

*My life always seemed so complicated when I was doing the PhD.
Peter, my husband, already had his PhD and was working in a research
job. He had always encouraged me as a mature age student and I
had struggled to balance the children's needs and my relationship
needs through those years. Then when I started the PhD I became
obsessed, I suppose, and I was unwilling to bend my needs around
those of the rest of the family. Although Peter understood my obsession
he somehow wanted things to just run along as they had before. We
struggled through and survived as a family, but I'm not sure how.*

—Maeling, a PhD graduate in Computer Science

For many students, starting a research degree marks the beginning of a new sense of academic freedom, with potential for personal creativity and reflection. At last you will be able to pursue an area of particular interest in depth. In most cases, you will not have the responsibilities associated with coursework. You will be free to structure your research and writing time, working when and where you want, with lots of time for thinking, reading, reflection and discussing issues in depth, generally immersing yourself in your area of study.

In some ways, your time for study will be more flexible, and you may be able to follow up some other interests which previously have not been possible due to course commitments. In the main, however, when you undertake postgraduate study you also have many other commitments, including family, other relationships, work, and so on. This chapter examines the situation in which many students find themselves—having multiple commitments and needing to rationalise and prioritise these in order to focus on their chosen research.

MAKING THE THESIS A TOP PRIORITY

When you enrol for a postgraduate degree by research, you are making a long-term commitment of time and energy. This commitment may involve a major reconsideration of priorities if you are to successfully complete your study within the normal time limits. You need to be clear about why you are engaging in postgraduate study and where study commitments will fit with the rest of your life goals, relationships and other demands. Recognising early that compromises may have to be made can be helpful in this process.

Case study

Peter had recently completed an honours degree very successfully and as a result was able to apply directly to enrol in a PhD program in his department. A senior lecturer with experience in his preferred thesis area was prepared to supervise him to undertake the PhD full time.

Peter's parents had assisted in supporting him to this stage but were now retiring from the workforce and were no longer able to assist financially. Peter preferred to study full time; however, he needed to support himself through some form of employment. He was offered a half-time tutoring position in an associated department, but that necessitated him studying part time, as he would need another outside job at night to support himself.

Another supervisor offered to supervise him in an industry-supported area. This would mean that he had to undertake a project largely defined by the industry supporter, and in return he would be employed two days a week thus earning sufficient money to support himself while still studying full time.

Peter was also a keen member of the local football team. He wanted to maintain this participation, but training conflicted with his working hours. He clearly had to decide what his highest priorities were and examine his options for financial survival.

There's no doubt that being excited about a topic is important, but the primary reason for undertaking research must be broader or else you will not survive the rigours of study at this level. Think carefully about why postgraduate study is important and how it fits with your overall 'life plan', if you have one.

Some students literally fall into postgraduate study because it seems to be a 'logical progression'. This may mark the beginning of a successful outcome, but it may also lead to disillusionment if you are not clear about what you are letting yourself in for. A study by Powles (1988) has suggested that having a clear idea of how the degree will facilitate your future career path is vital to clarifying priorities and maintaining motivation in the long term.

A strong commitment to research is also important. In order to give your work the attention required and to develop the motivation needed, your thesis needs to be given high priority in your life. However, it is vital to maintain balance by attending to physical fitness, recreational activities and relationships, as these also contribute to your long-term goals and will sustain you when the going gets tough. Some other pursuits may have to be given lower priority.

NEGOTIATING WITH FRIENDS, PARTNERS, CHILDREN AND SIGNIFICANT OTHERS

Case study

Joan returned to university to undertake a PhD at the age of 35 having worked in a variety of jobs, including teaching. She had three sons, all at high school, and the oldest was undertaking his final year. Her husband was a successful business manager, with a degree but no postgraduate qualifications. Joan previously worked part time and did most of the household management as well as driving her sons to various sporting commitments.

In order to undertake a PhD, she studied part time and reduced her working hours slightly. Although Joan and her husband had discussed the issue of her study and he had given her his support, she soon experienced conflicts over the household management and some resentment from her sons about her 'absence'. Her husband also noticed that suddenly she seemed distracted and had new commitments. He behaved in a jealous manner, questioning her about her connections at the university.

The above case study is a typical example of what might happen in a family, and in personal relationships, when one partner undergoes the dramatic change in role that taking on postgraduate study necessitates. Lack of prior discussion and knowledge about the amount of commitment required can be a significant hazard; however, it is difficult to predict at the beginning all the changes which might be involved. Joan's husband and sons needed to understand more clearly and accept her level of research commitments in order for the whole family to work out role changes which would suit all their needs.

There's no doubt that personal relationships can suffer as a result of the increased and altered commitments associated with postgraduate research. Think carefully about what is important to you and to others in your life. Any decision to undertake research at this level should be carefully negotiated with your partner or others who will be significantly affected by your decision.

For many students 'role absenteeism' in regard to close relationships is often the most critical issue. You may be accused of having changed. However, it is more likely that you are preoccupied and do not have the time or mental space to fulfil the roles in relationships which you have previously. Your partner may feel resentful of the time you spend at the university and with fellow students and academics. If your partner doesn't understand, or isn't sufficiently involved, they may even suspect that you are participating in some other 'extracurricular activity', not believing that anything else could occupy your attention to this extent. Ongoing conflicts in other areas of your life at this time will make your study task even more difficult. Feelings of guilt about the relationship or what other responsibilities you are neglecting at this time will only detract from your study.

Your partner should be encouraged to become aware of the commitments required. If possible, they should visit the school or department and attend any orientation sessions offered so that they can become aware of the environment in which you will be working and the demands made of you. Introduce them to other research students, their partners and friends. This will help them to realise they are not the only ones in this position and it will provide the opportunity for partners to develop their own support network. What is known and understood is often less of a threat than the unknown or misunderstood.

Talk about your work, involving your partner and others in the highs and lows. They are more likely to understand and support you in what you are doing. Remember that they have needs too, and you will need to work out compromises which suit both sides. If you perceive that relationship issues will be—or are already—a major problem for you, make an appointment to see a counsellor at the university in which you are enrolled.

Your time is valuable; think carefully about the most efficient and important use of it. For instance, uninterrupted 'together time' every week with your partner, children and others with whom you share your life should be a priority along with your study. Other things may provide important relaxation and recreational outlets. Some tasks may simply be time consuming and are better delegated to others.

SINGLE, UNATTACHED AND FREE OF COMMITMENTS?

Those students not involved in relationships, or who live alone, may be seen as having advantages in terms of less demands on their time and fewer competing roles to fulfil. However, the isolation of postgraduate study is a significant hazard and it may be difficult to maintain motivation without close supportive relationships. Networks of supportive friends and colleagues are therefore important. (Strategies for developing postgraduate support groups are outlined in chapter 7.)

It is vital to maintain a range of 'strings to your bow'. This means that in your life you need to have a number of important threads. These may include your postgraduate work, particular sporting interests, a particular group of friends, a part-time job, and so on. This means that when you are feeling low in relation to one area—for instance, your research is not working out—you have a number of other areas which are constant and affirming to help maintain your self-confidence. It is important that some of the other 'strings' (e.g. leisure activities, relationships) are independent of your postgraduate study. This diversity will counter a tendency for your self-esteem to be dependent on your sense of academic competence.

Case study

Joe was undertaking a PhD in Botany. He had accepted a place at a different university to that at which he had completed his undergraduate degree. However, he had tried to maintain some of his friendships from his undergraduate studies. He was in the university cricket team, which involved practice twice a week and games on Saturdays. At times he needed to find a replacement when his experiments required him to be in the lab on Saturday. Cricket provided him with a good physical outlet and a way to maintain fitness, as well as keeping in contact with a different group of students.

He also had a part-time teaching job at a local technical college, which involved working one night a week and some preparation time. He enjoyed the feedback from the students and, although it was sometimes difficult to prepare, he was also keeping his curriculum vitae active.

The students in the botany department were also quite social and went out for drinks regularly on a Friday night. Joe usually tried to attend as it was a good opportunity to let off steam and mix with other postgraduates socially.

Joe had some significant ups and downs in his postgraduate work. His supervisor transferred to another university and, although he was retained as a second supervisor, Joe had to establish a relationship with another supervisor in his present university. The new supervisor lacked knowledge in the area and power in the department, so Joe found it difficult at times to obtain the resources he needed for experiments.

Despite the challenges he faced with the competing demands on his time, Joe maintained the other 'strings' in his life and these assisted him to continue on when progress with his research was frustrating.

PRACTICAL REQUIREMENTS

You will need a space at home in which you can work undisturbed. An answering machine or voice mail can sometimes assist in managing telephone disruption if you can't take the phone off the hook. You need to be sure you have regular access to computer facilities either at home or in your department, if this is relevant. Discuss with others what forms of technology you can use to make life easier and more efficient. You need to negotiate uninterrupted time at home unless you have a study environment at your university to which you have unlimited access and you intend only to work at the university.

What postgraduate students say

What advice would you give other postgraduate students about managing work/family/academic demands?

- Set aside a specific amount of time each week and devote it to your research; a little time regularly will go a long way eventually.
- Be organised, set aside specific times to work.
- Make sure you take time out to relax and cater to your personal needs.
- Don't fret about your work, this wastes precious energy.
- Start putting the 'self' higher up in the family.
- Delegate.
- Let things like dusting and ironing go.
- Do study before chores.
- Learn not to be a perfectionist.
- Talk to your partner regularly about your research and the ups and downs.

You may need to get outside help to do certain tasks (e.g. mowing the lawn, housework, child-care). Most universities have employment officers who should be able to assist you to find others to do some of the jobs around the house which can be delegated. If you have older children, include them in the discussion and look at the possible extra roles they can fulfil. If you are in a shared house, negotiate with others and remember that unresolved conflicts over household tasks may take valuable time and energy from your study later if not handled well early on.

ROLES AND ASSOCIATED RELATIONSHIPS

When you are determining priorities, it can be useful to have a visual representation of the relationships which you have with others. A role diagram as described below provides one way to map your interactions. We all carry with us relationships from the past which may no longer be relevant or may be dysfunctional and even destructive in terms of our present life situation. This activity may help you to clarify your present situation and to determine which areas to change, develop or leave as they are.

Developing a role diagram

1. List your key roles and the people you deal with in those roles.

2. Evaluate each association with others. Decide whether it is likely to (a) help, (b) hinder or (c) remain neutral in regard to your present goals. Write down the specific ways in which this will happen.

3. Work out ways to maximise and minimise your contacts with the above according to whether they are helpful or harmful to your progress.

4. Repeat this process at least every six months. Do it more frequently if you find that conflicts and problems outside your study are affecting you to the extent that you are not making progress.

Figure 4.1 gives an example of a basic role diagram.

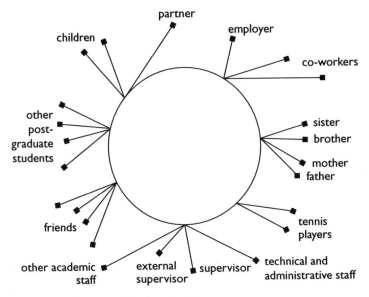

Figure 4.1 An example of a role diagram

chapter 5

Managing your time effectively

Well, for me just trying to cope with the day and night pressure of my research plus living a life was difficult. As a mature age student, the finishing stages were really hard. I had a baby, I had a husband, I had to cook meals and run a house. I think I'd advise other PhD students to get as much outside help as they can, particularly in the pressured times. I got friends and family to help with proofreading and I got some paid help in the house at times. I guess others use a network of people to help out.

—Ruth, a Masters student in Psychology

Postgraduate study normally offers you more flexibility in terms of time allocation than undergraduate study; however, most students begin their research with a variety of other seemingly less flexible commitments which also need to be managed and negotiated. Managing your time and commitments effectively becomes crucial to effective progress.

In many ways, as a postgraduate student you may have more flexible time than you have ever had before. You will need lots of this in order to think about issues, reflect and construct creative solutions; time for thinking and reflection is a vital part of postgraduate work. You will also need to be able to relax on occasions, and allow your 'subconscious' to work on problems and issues. For many students this happens best when they are focussing on other activities, such as recreation. Reflection tends to be easier if you are not tense, and this is more likely to be the case if you have a long-term plan which leaves you flexible but in control in the short term.

In order to develop an overall plan, you need to have an idea of what needs doing, and some sense of a time line for each area in order to complete the process in the desired time. You will need a great deal of flexibility in terms of time, coupled with a firm grasp of the stages you need to progress through. Although planning is primarily your responsibility, you should discuss these goals with your supervisor, taking advantage of their experience of the time needed for various tasks.

The first part of this chapter focusses on task isolation and time management. The second part focusses on identifying and dealing with procrastination, a common problem for many postgraduates during the planning, implementation and writing process.

SETTING A TIME FRAME

In order to set a time frame, you need to first identify all the activities you must undertake. You need to be as specific as possible. Obviously you will be clearer about the early tasks, while the later tasks will be broader and more difficult to specifically quantify in the early stages. The following is a list of initial tasks you may need to undertake:

- selecting a broad project area
- finding a supervisor
- selecting a thesis topic
- completing an initial literature review
- identifying a methodology
- identifying new skills required to carry out research
- designing a research program
- writing a thesis proposal

- seeking approval for the thesis proposal
- obtaining ethics clearance
- identifying other experts who may be needed for consultation
- locating or forming a student support group.

More advanced tasks include:

- writing the literature review
- carrying out a research program
- completing data analysis
- writing chapter drafts
- preparing illustrations
- distributing drafts for comment (supervisor, other specialists in the subject area, other students, friends)
- final drafts
- printing, binding, submission
- celebrating!

These lists are not exhaustive; every student will have different needs and requirements for their project. The second half of the list includes broader tasks which will be broken down and specified at a later stage.

Set out the required tasks on a long-term calendar. Every two to three months you should review your task list and adjust the time frame. Consult with your supervisor about appropriate time frames for the larger tasks. Also note on your calendar any periods when your supervisor will be away for large blocks of time, and thus unavailable for consultation, reading drafts, and so on.

Most students are optimistic in terms of their usage of time. That is, they expect that tasks will take less time than they actually do. Therefore it is a good idea to estimate a particular time for each task and then add one third to the time allowed. For instance, if you initially allow twelve days for writing a thesis proposal, then add four days (a third), making the time estimate sixteen days. This will also allow for unanticipated problems and hitches.

What postgraduate students say

How might you describe the personal demands involved in your experience of postgraduate study?

- I describe postgraduate study as both the hardest thing I've ever done and one of the most self-indulgent.
- Most days I feel fairly exhausted having to juggle my study, job and family. But I enjoy my research area and I persevere because I really want to finish and now it looks like I've almost made it. It's worth it!

What would you suggest to others?

- Stay fit to meet extra demands of energy needed.
- Enjoy a few fun/exercise sessions per week for yourself.
- Always work to an overall plan and rethink it every few months as you make progress.

Some students may need to have particular resources or develop special skills (foreign language, computer knowledge, data analysis programs). These are best addressed in the very early stages of your degree. For example, if you need to have the services of a statistician or another specialist with skills outside the range of your supervisor, then identify them early in the process. Arrange to meet with them to work out how and in what way they can work with you. Some students have more than one supervisor, or a board of supervisors with a chairperson; in other cases, students have consultants appointed by their department, which gives the specialist recognition as part of your supervision team.

Many students and supervisors advocate writing research papers along the way. This activity can provide you with the advantage of feedback on your research as you proceed. This will often come from acknowledged experts in your field of study. If you do decide to write and submit papers, allocate specific blocks of time for this purpose, but maintain a clear focus upon the final purpose of your research.

Keeping to a time frame is difficult at times, especially if you study part time and have family and work commitments. A regular review of your time frame will keep you alerted to changes in your progress and also provide an opportunity to allocate time more appropriately for your present needs.

What supervisors say about managing time

- There are many different styles of time management. Choose a style that suits you.
- There are supervisors who like to make weekly or fortnightly appointments, but I like students to take some initiative by setting meeting times when they need them.
- I think that by the time someone is doing a PhD they should not need a weekly appointment to keep their nose to the grindstone.
- You need to self-motivated, then the thesis is likely to be a success.

(Adapted from Cullen et al., 1994, pp. 50–65)

GETTING THINGS DONE

For some students, having a rigid timetable works; however, there's a risk of spending all your time *planning* what you will do instead of *doing* it. For most students it is more helpful to have a clear list of tasks and to gradually work through them, allowing yourself the flexibility to do tasks when it is appropriate, given their nature and urgency. Effective use of time is often most hindered by personal perceptions, attitudes and excuses for avoiding certain tasks.

The following points are useful for reviewing personal attitudes which may limit your effective use of time:

- *Take responsibility for your own decisions.* Think consciously about your use of time. If you make a decision to postpone a task, acknowledge it and acknowledge why you are doing it. Is it boredom, is making a decision too difficult or is something else more important?

- *You don't have to like doing it to get it done.* If you wait for the right moment to get started, you may never begin anything. Find a way that fits your present mood yet leads you towards rather than away from the task. Focus on completion of the task, how it will feel. Take the 'swiss cheese' approach: tackle any part of the task which appeals to you, just to get started.
- *Getting started leads to involvement.* Don't bank on or wait for large chunks of uninterrupted time. They are rarely available, so use small amounts of time to begin. Gather momentum by getting started and becoming involved even in a small way. Once you are engaged the project itself exerts a stronger and stronger pull. Setting yourself to work initially in short and strictly limited bursts means that getting started is not the beginning of an endless experience.
- *Make your goals reachable.* Define your goal in action terms so that you know when you have achieved it, e.g. 'I'll make an appointment with my supervisor today'. Keep your goals manageable and specific rather than abstract or utopian, e.g. 'I am going to write an introductory paragraph today' rather than 'I am going to turn over a new leaf'. Tackle goals step by step. You can't be there without first having been en route. There are rewards to be had from the process of getting there. Revise your goals in the light of realistic constraints so that they are actually possible.
- *Induce action.* Put what needs doing in the middle of your desk where it can't be overlooked. Visualise the steps you will take and yourself in action to make it easier to cross the threshold between thinking and doing. The more detailed your plan, the more likely it is that action will follow. List the benefits of completing the task to give yourself an incentive to act. Reinforce any progress you make along the way. These are important steps towards completion of the task. To keep yourself involved set the

next step ahead of time so that you know what you will pick up when you come back to the task.

- *Watch out for signs of procrastination.* Recognise excuses, which are red flags denoting a choice point: to procrastinate or to act. Redefine difficulties as challenges to be mastered. Set yourself up to succeed by optimising the circumstances in which you make your first move. Pick conditions that will work for you, not against you. Don't let obstacles bring you to a grinding halt. An obstacle is just an obstacle, not a signal to abandon all effort. Allow for things to go wrong at the last minute, for interruptions and disruption. Recognise your own perfectionism. It is more important that things are done than that they are perfect, that is, it is important to act, not to act flawlessly.

Time Management Matrix

This matrix (Figure 5.1), proposed by Stephen Covey (1990), can be used to determine priorities when ordering conflicting tasks. Tasks are assigned according to their urgency and their importance in your overall scheme.

Urgency

		High	Low
Importance	**High**	e.g. crisis	e.g. relationship-building, postgraduate research tasks, writing
	Low	e.g. interruptions, phone calls	e.g. television

Figure 5.1 Allocation of time

Urgent means it requires immediate attention. Urgent matters are usually visible. They press on us, they insist on action. They are often popular with others. *Importance* has to do with results. If something is important, it contributes to your mission, your values and your high priority goals.

The second quadrant, that is, high on importance and low on urgency, is the heart of effective personal time management. It deals with things that are not urgent, but are important. These are often the tasks which we leave until last, dealing instead with the urgent but unimportant tasks.

HOW TO AVOID PROCRASTINATION

Postgraduate study differs from undergraduate study in that there are few intermediate deadlines. This means that you control the pace of work and, to start with, the time in which you must complete your thesis seems infinite. This is an illusion, and the risk of saying 'Tomorrow will be soon enough to make a start' is greatly increased. As you begin to find your feet in postgraduate study, lack of confidence at this academic level may also make you reluctant to act. You may feel that you do not know the rules and standards which are applied at this level and thus you become reluctant to put pen to paper or to take actions which might demonstrate the standard you are able to operate at.

Sometimes being too busy is the same thing as procrastinating. By piling on commitments you may be setting the stage for procrastination and providing yourself with a ready excuse. You may need to ask yourself what irrelevant things you can give up for your most important goals. Being available to others, because it seems so justified, is a deceptive kind of procrastination. Being so ready to respond to the demands of others leaves you short of time to attend to your own responsibilities. Your feeling of being needed and being indispensable becomes a cloak for temporising.

Students who procrastinate may find it easier to respond to undue pressure, whether internal or external, by simply not trying. It may seem safer to procrastinate and never take the risk of not making it if they feel any doubts about meeting their own or others' expectations. The trouble is that success is frequently defined in terms of perfection. Confronted with such impossibly high and unrealistic standards they may run for the cover of procrastination.

In order to guard against this potential pitfall it makes sense to reflect on any prior history of using delaying tactics, and to consider the purpose procrastination may have served for you in your life. If all else fails, procrastinate positively. Sit in a chair for five minutes and do absolutely nothing. It is a strategy that will almost certainly bring you back to the scheduled task raring to go. Remember, procrastination is the art of making the possible thing impossible.

Other brief pointers for overcoming procrastination include:

- Segment your tasks.
- Recognise when you work most productively and take advantage of your prime time.
- Set up a specific time for the task. If you have not achieved a task by the time specified, move on to the next task.
- Eliminate 'should' from your vocabulary.
- Be aware and beware of perfectionism.
- Tell someone else of your commitment.

- Change your surroundings.
- Write yourself reminders.
- Have your own reward and penalty system.
- Work on only one task at a time.
- Ask others for help.
- Make a permanent 'to do' list.
- Recognise your own style.
- Talk to yourself in a positive way.

POSITIVE DECISION MAKING

A good decision is one which is made clearly, with the benefit of appropriate research and without regret. In regard to your research and thesis it is always a good idea to document important decisions, noting why you took a particular direction and recording the options you discounted and why. This may relate to a particular topic or an approach. Some of that information may be necessary for your thesis justification and sometimes you may need to refer to it at a later stage to remind yourself that you did the right thing. In order to avoid regret it is important to let go of other options when you make the decision and, if necessary, mourn their loss or acknowledge that that is another path which you can take up later.

chapter 6

The research thesis rollercoaster

Some of the highlights have been going to conferences and getting feedback on my work. I think the low times come from the daily grind—the way it's so drawn out and just seems to be without deadlines, and no section of it is ever finished ... It never feels as if anything is complete and it seems to accumulate forever.

—Daniel, a PhD student in Arts

You have committed yourself, perhaps without knowing it, to a period of intense highs and lows. Life generally consists of highs and lows mediated with straight patches. While you are undertaking research and writing the thesis, it is likely that within any week you will experience intense excitement and satisfaction, and dismal failure. You may also have periods in the doldrums when you contemplate throwing it all in. At other times you may feel plain bored and need to reassess why you are where you are. During more extreme moments, you may become quite introspective and ask questions of yourself in terms of: 'Who am I?' All of this is quite normal behaviour for postgraduate students. However, it is common for students to wonder at times if they are going mad and why they ever put themselves on this path.

Some students talk about the three 'd's—depression, doubt and desperation—which occur along with bouts of enjoyment and elation. Other students might experience what feels like 'temporary insanity' during the thesis stage. The highs and lows certainly can bring about obsessive or anti-social behaviours which are not normally characteristic of the individual. Talking about these feelings with others who are going through a similar process or who have finished their postgraduate study will help you to understand and clarify what's happening to you. As one PhD student noted: 'Your thesis almost seems to acquire a life of its own … it's a bit like having a relationship with another person—it can be so unpredictable and frustrating.'

There is also the 'post-thesis completion trough' or 'post-partum blues' which many students experience. It's a bit like having prepared for years and then finally climbed Mount Everest only to be left wondering, 'What do I do now?'

COMMON DOUBTS OF RESEARCH STUDENTS

Many students have negative feelings and thoughts, and it is useful to examine the rational basis for these in order to deal with them. Such thoughts can sabotage your research if they are not recognised as normal and dealt with appropriately. The following points are adapted from Sternberg, 1981.

I've picked the wrong topic

Having worked through a very thorough proposal and having had it accepted, you can assure yourself that you have not picked the wrong topic. You are simply undermining yourself—typical self-sabotaging behaviour—and should recognise that this is one of those troughs in the thesis process which will pass. Re-read your proposal to remind yourself that you are on track and to confirm the direction in which you are heading. Re-read your journal, which should have listed the reasons why you discarded other topics and chose this one.

The data have come out wrong

There's a problem if you have too much invested in results turning out a particular way. Lack of openness to possibilities and flexibility in hypothesis testing can be a danger. Talk it out with your supervisor and others.

I just can't write anything, whatever I do nothing comes

Most students experience some degree of 'writer's block' many times during the writing process. It doesn't mean that you won't be able to finish; it is a temporary situation, a bit like a car stalling. You need to recognise that writing is difficult and challenging and, talking to others, you will realise that this happens to everyone. Writing needs to become a habit, something you do routinely every day throughout your research process.

When you are truly blocked, it's a good idea to write down what you feel about your thesis. Get those emotions going and you may find that your writing begins to flow again. Try doing some reading on related areas and increase the amount of conversations about your topic. You could ask your supervisor for an extra meeting to talk about where you are at. Explain the problem and talk about it. This is usually not the time to take a long break from your thesis as you may come back feeling even colder towards the idea than before. Like a stalled car, leaving it parked in the garage for a week or more may make the problem worse.

The end is so far away, I've got so much to do, I don't think I can finish

Writing a thesis can be a little like bushwalking; when you expect to come to the top of a hill and see a view, you find that you are at the crest of a minor hill and the mountain is much further off in the distance. Reflect on what you have achieved so far. Try to set goals which are manageable in the short term. Look at the steps you need to take to get to the larger goal. Break the tasks up as much as possible and focus only on the short term for a while. For example, what you need to do in the next week. Set a reward for yourself for having completed certain small tasks.

This isn't good enough—it should be perfect

Many students believe that their thesis should be perfect, flawless, the best thing they have ever done or will ever do. No thesis is ever perfect. No matter how much effort you put in, there is always something that could have been done differently or better. That does not mean that you should not aim to do your best. One of the arts to researching and writing a thesis is to recognise and acknowledge boundaries. There are always limits to what is required, necessary or appropriate for your project. This is not the last and only thing you will do, so it does not have to be an absolutely perfect representation of your talents.

For some students it can seem that their whole life's worth can hang on their thesis. This is also why it is important to have other 'strings to your bow', other activities and relationships which are independent of your thesis process and remind you of your worth and talents.

I've left something out, or I haven't accounted for ...

Students often lose their perspective and believe that everyone else knows as much about the topic as they do. They perceive that everyone knows about all the minute holes in the work that they themselves recognise. In reality, markers and assessors will see the same large gaping holes that your supervisor has seen, but they will not be as intimately connected with the topic as you are and thus won't see or know it in the intricate way that you do. You do need to account for and articulate clearly the reasons why you have chosen this method rather than another, why this or that happened, and so on. In writing you need to be able to place limits on the work so that the reader's expectations are given boundaries also.

NEGATIVE FEELINGS ABOUT YOURSELF

I'm not up to the task; there's no way I'll be able to pull this thing together

It is common to doubt your decision to undertake this level of research. That's why a journal can be useful, especially if you record your initial decision-making processes. Chart the course of your decision to begin this project and then the decisions about the topic as you go along, indicating how you discounted other topics and why you settled on this one. With any decision, especially one as large as this, it is common to later question the wisdom of taking it on. Remind yourself that your decision was the right one at the time and that you sorted through the options thoroughly then. You have been accepted to study at this level, which means that others also have faith in your ability and your past performance indicates your competence. It is generally recognised that there is prob-ably a base level of ability which is required to complete a Masters or doctorate by research. The other, more significant, component of success is persistence and determination to follow through, despite seemingly insurmountable challenges. As one successful PhD candidate put it: 'My overriding feeling was that it was a test of endurance and determination rather than ability. I got through because of my refusal to contemplate any alternative to finishing.'

Why am I doing this? Why am I enduring this pain?

If you have kept a journal, then you should look back at the reasons why you chose to go through this process. A sense of 'no end in sight' is a common feeling. This can be exacerbated by well-meaning friends and relatives who see your struggle, wonder why you are doing it and may even try to persuade you to give up. They are often not aware of the highs and lows you are likely to experience and, although they are well meaning, they haven't been there, so really have no idea what you are going through. Surround yourself with supportive, understanding friends who can be positive and constructive when you talk about the process. You are better off talking to other candidates, your supervisor and other staff who have done postgraduate study. Pain is a common part of the process and it is not so much masochistic as functional in these circumstances.

If I ever finish this, I'll never write another thing in my life

Thesis 'burnout' is common in postgraduate students. The fact is that your thesis is the beginning of the next step in your career path. This may go in a number of directions but most likely will involve the writing of articles and/or a book for publication, as well as other writing tasks which will further your cause and help to disseminate your research. Believing that it will be the last thing you ever write can also help fuel the belief that your thesis must be perfect. This is an unrealistic expectation which will sabotage your ability to complete it at all. Try to focus on the short term for a while, on positive perceptions of completion: how it will feel, how you will celebrate, and so on.

THE UPS AND DOWNS OF THE RESEARCH WAVES

Many people identify common ups and downs in the research and thesis process which can be depicted as a series of waves and troughs that can be anticipated, though not necessarily in exactly the same sequence or at the same time for every student.

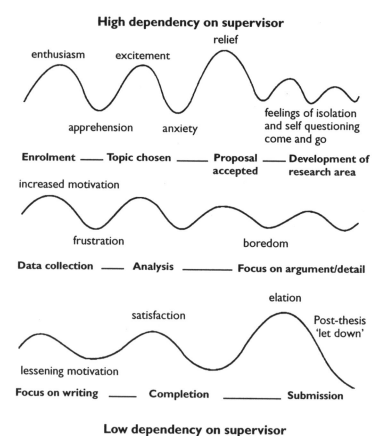

Figure 6.1 The ups and downs of research

Throughout the whole process, there is little doubt that it is vital to keep focussed on what you want to achieve, and why. There will be significant hurdles (or, more precisely, brick walls) to scale and you will need tenacity and determination to eventually get there.

Try always to surround yourself with reminders of your own competence. Practise reassuring yourself by reiterating your strengths. Mix with others who understand the process and will give you positive support when you need it.

(chapter 7)

Maintaining motivation and getting support

I try to have contact with people around me who are interested in my work. Unfortunately, I cross two disciplines, so I can easily get feedback on the education side but not on the film side. But I do still think that constant contact and just having people around who will occasionally listen to the obsession that you develop with your topic helps.

—Judith, a PhD student in Media Studies

I think postgraduate study can be a solitary experience, so establishing links with people in similar academic areas and going to conferences and seminars is very important. Talking to friends and fellow students who have actually finished also reassures you that it can be done, as opposed to it being some kind of abstract achievement, an abstract goal that you might or might not reach.

—Neil, a PhD student in Law

The most challenging aspect of postgraduate study is maintaining motivation and completing the task which you have set for yourself. Potential employers of postgraduates have argued that their reason for employing someone with postgraduate qualifications may not simply be knowledge of the person but, more importantly, evidence that the candidate is able to develop, implement and complete a large and personally demanding task. Some of the most important personal attributes underlying success are not intellectual acumen, creativity, or even originality, but rather tenacity, which is based on maintaining motivation. In this chapter we will focus on two strategies to assist you to maintain motivation throughout your candidature: keeping a journal and taking advantage of peer support.

Maintaining motivation throughout your postgraduate candidature is clearly your responsibility. At times it may be the most difficult aspect of the process, as your success or notable achievements are not immediately obvious and the tedious aspects of completion result in boredom. Your interactions with your supervisor and other students undergoing similar processes will assist you to retain your focus. The speed and impetus of the process will vary considerably according to the stage you are at and your own personal style and circumstances.

For many postgraduates keeping a journal or diary of the process can assist to maintain focus and a sense of direction and motivation in the longer term. Frequent contact with other postgraduate students can help you to manage the ups and downs inherent in postgraduate research and also gain important alternative perspectives for your research.

KEEP A JOURNAL

Your journal can be used, as described in chapter 5, to assist you with time management and the planning of a time frame for completion of tasks and stages. More importantly, your journal can be used to maintain a record of your research process. In your journal you should document all major decisions and the reasons for them. This will help when you want to reflect back on why you took one path rather than another. For instance, you may decide to limit the scope of your research by omitting a particular area, or you may decide to move in a different direction altogether. Write down the reasons why you did this;

you will then be able to refer to them when you describe your rationale in your thesis. Sometimes we can later reflect on a decision and tend to be regretful if we cannot clearly remember the rationale we used when we made it.

Use your journal to note all achievements and highs, no matter how insignificant. Celebrate every one in some way. (There's no need to list all the downs; you won't have any trouble remembering them.) It may be solving a particular problem in the research, acquiring a new skill, writing a page or a whole chapter, depending on where you are in the process. There is a strong tendency for postgraduate students to simply feel relieved when they complete a task and to focus on the next challenge immediately, rather than acknowledging that progress has been made. One way to celebrate your progress is to share it with other postgraduate students. This can be on an informal basis or at organised group meetings.

PEER SUPPORT OR SUPERVISORY GROUPS FOR STUDENTS

Students working at postgraduate level often form casual support groups to enable them to share and enjoy the process, or simply to survive its rigours. When they are informal such groups can be seen as simply peer support, however, if they are organised formally and meet regularly, they can become supervisory groups which provide an adjunct to the supervision provided by a supervisor.

Informally, a group of postgraduate students in a faculty or department may decide to meet once a week at a particular place, perhaps for a drink or a meal. If you are in a department with a postgraduate students' common room, you may be able to meet regularly with other students who frequent the area. Or your university may have a postgraduate students' association which organises regular social events. In each of these cases, such get-togethers can fulfil an important need for social contact with others in a similar situation to yourself.

Many postgraduate students, however, find it beneficial to

have a more formally organised meeting with other students which focusses on research issues, while providing social support as well. There are a variety of bases for such a group. A group may be set up by students who are using the same methodology on different types of projects. They may agree to meet regularly and use an informal structure to share information about their progress and give each other support and encouragement.

Alternatively, two or three supervisors working in the same faculty may choose to set up a group for the students they supervise, even if they are working in different content areas with different methodologies. One or more of the supervisors might regularly attend the group's meetings to provide advice and assistance. The group could consist of, say, ten students who agree to meet to provide each other with a forum for presenting material on their progress. The group meeting could replace one of the normal supervisory sessions.

There are clearly many combinations of circumstances which may be appropriate for setting up and operating a peer support or supervisory group. In order to maintain such a group and make it successful in the longer term, it is usually necessary to pay attention to the basic principles of group functioning.

How to maintain an effective group

The following guidelines may assist in maximising and maintaining the effectiveness of your support or supervisory group:

- It is helpful, but not essential, for participating students to be working in a similar or related area. This sense of common purpose ensures some level of understanding of each other's issues.
- The optimum size of a group is six to eight members, if all attend regularly. With weekly meetings, members only have to wait about a month to present their work to the group.
- Meetings should be held on a regular basis, such as weekly

or fortnightly, with a strong commitment to attend. This ensures that members get an audience and support whenever they present material.

- Meetings need to have some structure, however loose, which is adhered to in order to maintain focus. Having a chairperson for each meeting may assist this.
- Try to maintain a specific location and regular time for the meeting. This ensures that members remember to attend and have it as part of their schedule.
- Members can take turns to present work in progress, or ideas for which they need a sounding board. Socialisation should be separate from the work aspect of the meeting; socialise either before or after the meeting, or at a different time. Time should be allowed to 'celebrate' individual members' successes.
- Guests might be invited to cover a particular area of interest or a common problem for the whole group.
- If trust is to be developed between members, then some agreement needs to be reached about sharing confidential or sensitive material at meetings.

Advantages of supervisory groups

There are many advantages for both students and supervisors in the formation of such groups:

- Students give and receive personal support to and from each other. This tends to assist students to be more independent and thus reduces demands on supervisors.
- Students can often provide some supervisory assistance to each other, thus reducing the need for direct contact with the supervisor.
- Group membership increases motivation among students.
- Students help each other to learn. Explanations are from a student perspective and thus for some may be easier to grasp.
- Students are exposed to a wider range of research questions and processes.

- Students are involved in a research culture, which creates opportunities for collaborative research.
- There is a greater likelihood of students succeeding, which increases the job satisfaction for the supervisor.
- Opportunities exist for students to rehearse proposals and presentations.
- Group meetings and goal setting encourage students to maintain their time frame.
- Peer support is available for students passing through difficult stages.

As pressure increases on supervisors of postgraduate students to maintain an increasing number of roles within university departments and faculties, they are likely to be less accessible to students. As a result, postgraduate students will need to become more self-reliant and have alternative sources of academic support. This being the case, student supervisory groups are likely to become more essential to student progress and completion.

What postgraduate students say

What advice would you offer to fellow postgraduate students about to embark on postgraduate study?

- Keep in touch with fellow students who are 'in the same boat'. Meet regularly with them. Keep up motivation and interest at all costs.
- Think carefully about the huge undertaking you are about to embark on; it will involve some sacrifices on your part if you are to succeed. You need to *want* to do it—this will give you the necessary push along the way.
- Try not to be discouraged by family members or work demands.
- Be sure the research topic is appropriate given your background knowledge in the field.

Thesis design and construction

I think I designed my study particularly badly. Perhaps that's a problem with a qualitative research project. What I found particularly unhelpful was being constantly forced to try and write a theoretical chapter that I couldn't seem to get in order. I suppose it's that division between the theory and the practical and I'm not sure that in every case the theory is the best way to do it.

—Zachariah, a PhD student in Landscape Architecture

This chapter is concerned with guiding principles in successfully writing a thesis, while chapter 9 takes up the practical issues of revising, editing and proofreading your text.

Using writing effectively will not only enhance the knowledge, findings and interpretations in your thesis, but will also assist you, through careful drafting and redrafting, to solve the problems you will inevitably face as the project unfolds. Such problems are not merely to do with expression, but also with understanding, and through the skilful use of writing you will develop a more successful thesis.

PAST SKILLS STILL APPLY

Although the research degree is probably the most extensive and distinctive academic project that you will undertake as a student, skills learned in earlier degree studies continue to apply. These skills consist of being:

- relevant in your approach
- persuasive in your use of evidence
- objective in your presentation
- accurate and discriminating in your documentation.

A successful thesis also demonstrates the other skill of effective writing: producing text which is clear, convincing and interesting to the reader. This involves, as it does for all writers, drafting and redrafting so that you get the precise effects that you want in the text of the thesis.

WRITING THE THESIS OCCURS IN A DISTINCTIVE CONTEXT

The written thesis is the external representation of all the work that you have done in its preparation. The major challenges are:

- arriving at a sustainable and relevant argument
- developing a research paradigm which will provide a productive and valid method for executing the project
- successfully applying the methodologies of the thesis
- efficiently organising the resources for the study
- developing a structure for the thesis which effectively underpins its exposition and defence
- undertaking a literature review which will demonstrate both the singular contribution of the thesis and your scholarly mastery of the broad field of specialist knowledge in which your thesis is placed.

From this perspective the thesis is not narrow and specialised but an enterprise of considerable intellectual breadth. In short, the basic goals are to deliver a scholarly piece of work whose distinctiveness and intellectual substance will be recognised, and appreciated, by experts in the field. As well, the higher degree thesis will not be seen as an end in itself, but a sustained occasion where the skills of research are so soundly developed that you could, if you wish, embark upon a research career. This must be delivered through writing which presents your study with admirable clarity, and makes its innate interest and importance clear to your readers. Writing is the medium and it must act to enhance, not detract, from what will be a complex and intensive project. If carefully conducted, the thesis is also likely to be a rewarding experience both intellectually and personally.

Good writing will be facilitated by your intimate knowledge of the topic. You will want to write, and this intellectual confidence in the thesis will drive your writing on. By contrast, you will sometimes have read material which lacks intellectual confidence, and where the writer as a result:

- tends to fudge the issues
- fails to explore linkages
- seems unaware of the implications of what is written or the questions which can quite legitimately be asked of the text, but for which there seem to be no answers to hand
- has drifted away from the case which is being presented.

It is probably wise to run a check over your written work to ensure that none of the above weaknesses is evident.

How, then, can you reach a point of writing efficiency where your text admirably serves your thesis?

YOUR RESEARCH FORMS THE FOUNDATION FOR EFFECTIVE WRITING

Writing, no matter how well it is technically executed, will not automatically deliver a good thesis. Rather, writing is the outward manifestation of all that you know, and your appreciation of the complexities and implications of your investigation. Effective thesis writing is, therefore, underpinned by the various features indicated at the beginning of the chapter. Nevertheless, do not see writing as divorced from your study, the cosmetic result of all that you do. Quite the contrary; writing will be extremely important throughout the thesis in testing your ideas and thesis structure on the screen (or paper). At *the last stage* of writing, the final draft should be so effectively written that it greatly enhances your project. Writing must never be permitted to detract from the quality of your thesis and its defence.

DO NOT DELAY THE COMMENCEMENT OF WRITING

Try to avoid putting off the commencement of writing—for example, until 'all the results are in'. Delay is likely to weaken and protract thesis delivery. It is appreciated that the specific research and results of your project are the focal part of your work, and much effort will go into gaining them. Nevertheless, they do not enjoy a life independent of the thesis to the extent that other aspects can await their completion. It is essential that you:

- use writing quite early to refine your thesis
- become highly aware of the central issue that you are researching
- articulate a rationale for your investigation
- develop a rigorous argument.

If this is not done, your research and your writing generally may lack focus, a major complaint of examiners when assessing theses. By contrast, if you do this as early as practicable, and then restate as necessary in the light of subsequent research, reading and reflection, your project will possess clear orientation and goals. Studies of higher degree research students indicate that those who develop a clear statement of the central issue early on, know where they are going and have sustainable goals for the thesis, finish successfully and without undue waste of time.

In particular, do not fall into the trap of setting unrealistic goals for yourself—these make the thesis unnecessarily burdensome and delay submission. Your major goals for the thesis and the extent of work likely to be involved should be discussed with your supervisor. You may wish to get other external reactions to your project's intention by discussing it with other possible audiences (such as a co-supervisor, other relevant members of staff, and postgraduate students in the area).

Your project's contribution to knowledge may come from one or more sources:

- it could be the special nature of the sample you use in your investigation
- your methodologies might be distinctive within the context of your investigation
- you may be researching a specific problem that has not been examined before
- your thesis may challenge established interpretations
- you may extend already researched activities
- you may be able to make new discoveries.

Whatever its distinctive contributions, it must demonstrate your effectiveness as a researcher, your familiarity with the relevant field of knowledge, and the informed placement of your thesis within that field of knowledge.

KEEP YOUR LITERATURE REVIEW UP TO DATE

You must also commence writing up, or recording in some other suitable way, the results of your ongoing literature review. This is a task of considerable importance to the thesis. Through it you master the relevant area of knowledge, and hence have the background to present a critically informed study. It also enables you to gain a clearer and more substantial focus on the distinctive contribution that will be made by your project. The literature review may yield significant methodologies for your study, and certainly major theories, interpretations or conclusions. You will become aware of conflicting schools of thought (or interpretation or theoretical position) and how they impinge upon your work. The literature review will enable you to write the discussion and conclusion sections of your thesis with an informed critical background from which to emphasise the significance of the results of your project.

The literature review is likely to be a continuing task as you try to unravel the more complex theories and their relevance to your thesis. You may undertake some exploration in related disciplinary areas. You will also want to keep abreast of the most recent state of knowledge in your field. It is not suggested, therefore, that the literature review should be completed early. Nevertheless, substantial early written work on it is essential to the project. Try also to keep some clear bounds on your literature review so that it does not become too broad and involved. Constantly test the relevance of your reading and consequent writing to your thesis.

BE AWARE OF COPING STRATEGIES

As discussed in chapter 6, it is not uncommon for research degree students to become overwhelmed by the seemingly vast extent of their projects. However, there are various strategies which will help you to keep it in focus. First of all, the clear statement of your thesis and its rationale should enable you to keep control over material, including the relevance of research data. Read, write and research with your thesis statement forever before you.

Appreciate as well that while the project and the work involved may seem vast, it is in fact divided into smaller and, therefore, more manageable pieces. These sections of the thesis are obviously interrelated but each requires different emphases and skills. This should bring variety and greater manageability to your work. The literature review engages you in a synthesis and evaluation of the work of others. The methods section enables you to display much initiative in the methodologies you adopt, the research data you collect, and how you analyse it. The results section gives you the opportunity of making the outcomes of your empirical or qualitative study clear to your readers. The discussion chapter enables you to emphasise the distinctiveness of your investigation, particularly in relation to the field of knowledge traversed in your literature review. The conclusion enables you to restate legitimate claims for your thesis as well as its contribution to a field of knowledge. And each of these major divisions, notably the literature review and the methods chapters, will be divided into smaller interrelated units. In total, however, your thesis will be a unity with considerable 'cross talk' (relating one chapter to another) across its various sections.

The nature of your text will also change within a chapter according to your goals. On some occasions your paragraphs will explain or define, on others they will present evidence and analyse. In some paragraphs you will engage in an evaluation of work previously undertaken in the field, in others you will discuss or report results. An appreciation of the rich variety in the text of a thesis should dispel impressions that you are engaged in a comparatively unvarying task. Try to closely analyse examples of different types of discourse that occur in the articles and monographs that you read as exemplars for your own writing.

It is not uncommon for research degree students to experience 'mid-thesis blues'. Temporary feelings of negativity probably accompany most extensive projects. Nevertheless, they can be alleviated, in a research degree project, by a clear focus on where you are heading, a plan which allows you to make noticeable progress with the thesis, and an appreciation of its innate variety.

WRITING SHOULD SERVE YOU POWERFULLY IN THE DEVELOPMENT OF YOUR THESIS

Try to avoid being in a hurry to get to the final written version of each chapter. Instead, see drafting and redrafting as powerful instruments in producing a good thesis. Your early writing or drafting will inform you of what you know and do not know. This will be one of its most helpful attributes. As you write you may be surprised at the ideas and insights that are occurring to you. Some of them might be very good, others, in the cold light of day, might need some reshaping or might ultimately be rejected. But this written exploration is vital to the intellectual worth of your thesis.

WRITING SHOULD AID THINKING AND THE MASTERY OF KNOWLEDGE

When you undertake such tasks as paraphrasing or summarising, the act of expression in your own words signals that you are mastering the material, including its complexities and the nature of its interpretation (or expressed meaning).

Writing in the service of the writer is a vital part of your intellectual journey in writing a thesis. This is sometimes referred to as 'writer-centred' text. It is not meant for the reader, but for you to try to clarify your thoughts and conceptual understanding in preparing the thesis. This is private writing, confident and experimental, away from supervisors, examiners and readers, where you can try out your ideas, critically examine your insights, and make trial runs. It is also a time when you can wrestle with the implications of your thesis, or evaluate the interpretations of the specialists in your field, measuring the sustainability of their arguments and evidence and its relationship to your thesis.

Although drafting and redrafting is essentially a private affair, some supervisors have reported excellent results by occasionally making writing more public and corporate. The mentor (or supervisor) meets with three or four research degree students working in related areas. Together they discuss and draft written responses (the supervisor included) to a problem being experienced by a member of the group. The written results are then discussed. This approach seems invaluable, particularly when you are having difficulty articulating a major interpretation and its significance to your thesis, or enunciating a strong case for a particular methodology which you are going to adopt, or expressing the connection between a philosophical position and your thesis.

SEE WRITING AS AN EVOLUTIONARY ACT

You should avoid viewing writing solely as end product without its other function as an intermediate or evolutionary process. Undue focus on the final draft, on the flawlessness of the final written product, can inhibit the development of your project. It is difficult to achieve orderly, insightful, technically perfect prose from the very beginning. Proofreading an early draft as you write may slow down the thinking process. This may require perceiving mistakes or weaknesses as learning or recasting opportunities. In the final thesis they will be notably absent, but in the meantime they may be evolutionary steps on the road to perfection.

DON'T BE FEARFUL OF WRITING

The more relaxed yet diligent you are in your writing, the more successful you are likely to be. Exploit the positive things your supervisor has to say about your writing, and move to strengthen those aspects which are less positive. Again, just about all of us have certain idiosyncrasies in our writing of which we should be aware and ready to correct. They can be as diverse as overusing certain expressions to constantly writing overly long sentences, becoming unduly assertive and seemingly unbending in written statements, or being repetitious or verbose. Writing is, to some extent, an unconscious act and these personal predilections enter our text almost unwittingly. The great remedy is your critical eye during the redrafting process.

It is not surprising that research students often experience undue anxiety about writing. Writing is a public act and all its imperfections are apparent to the aware reader. It is not uncommon to find that undergraduate students are loath to re-read what they have written. They then commit the fatal error of submitting a first draft as their final essay. Perhaps this fear has been deepened by the unbalanced emphasis that is given to errors in the surface aspects of text—that is, grammar, usage and punctuation. In brief, writing seems to be an error-ridden enterprise. Of course, it often is, *through the drafts*—and there's the rub. If the drafts are constructively used for correcting weaknesses of substance and editing weaknesses of expression, and the penultimate draft for correcting technical errors, much of this fear of errors in the final draft should disappear.

LEARN FROM SUCCESSFUL ACADEMIC WRITERS

How do accomplished academic writers achieve text of high effectiveness? Are they so skilled that the tasks of revision (in which the substance of the work is reviewed), editing (where the revised draft is made completely comprehensible to the reader) and proofreading are achieved even as they write their work? No, they are not. The most accomplished writers undertake careful reviews of their writing, and professional writers often employ an editor as well as a proofreader to assist them with the task. Indeed, research suggests that those accomplished writers who seem to do little reviewing or rewriting have in fact thoroughly rehearsed what they are going to write before they commence.

You will know of examples of successful writing in your field. The most effective writers warrant close analysis. This includes an appreciation of the way their work is structured and expressed so that it is interesting and accessible. It is worth reflecting on why these researchers are regarded as leaders in the field. You will also have the benefit of reading completed Masters or PhD theses and deciding why some are considered successful. These are experiences that should make you aware in a tangible way of what is required for the research degree for which you are studying.

TRY TO ACHIEVE SCHOLARLY DETACHMENT

Try to maintain a detached distance from your work so that it retains balance, breadth of vision and objectivity. Reference is sometimes made to the third eye—that is, your capacity to read your work with an eye rather than your own: a reader's eye. This is not merely a matter of testing writing style or editorial effectiveness. It is a readiness to ask of your text the questions that a reader would ask, and satisfy yourself that these questions have been effectively answered in your writing.

Occasionally, some research degree students become somewhat fixated on their theses. It is not difficult to see why this occurs, since so much time is invested in the project and so much is known about it. But it is not a constructive perspective. It can affect the writer's assessment of the work and result in too narrow a view. It may also lead to the rejection of sound criticism and the loss of an open-minded scholarly view. This is unfortunate, for once the thesis is submitted and enters the public domain, it must be able to sustain the most rigorous critical enquiry.

Sometimes the problem may be not so much a matter of undue defensiveness as a genuine belief that some sections of writing are much better than they actually are. This happens to many writers, and is probably a product of the intimacy of the writing task. That is, it may be hard to achieve perspective after you have been writing for a considerable period. These are the times when you need a break from writing, and should take up other tasks related to the thesis. When you return, you should be able to assess your work more clearly.

AVOID UNDUE ABSTRACTION

As your study unfolds you will acquire a highly specialised knowledge of your field. Because you want to express its complications and/or because you are so close to it, you may have a tendency to express yourself in too abstract a manner or too densely. By contrast, clarity of expression demonstrates to the reader that you understand the concepts you are exploring, as well as making your writing easier to read. Therefore, being ready to restate material more clearly should be a part of the redrafting task. Your completed thesis should be able to be read and appreciated by an educated person who is not a specialist in the field.

Undue abstraction may also come from the other direction —a lack of understanding of the theories, key concepts or methodological positions that are an integral part of the field of study. Lack of understanding therefore leads to misuse of terms or opaque, confused text.

Your vocabulary transmits the message of your thesis, so be completely at ease with the terms you use. The use of specialist dictionaries or glossaries in your discipline should assist your work. You may wish to purchase a paperback edition of a well-recognised dictionary in your discipline and supplement it with the more extensive discipline dictionaries in the reference section of the university library. The development of your own glossary of terms, perhaps in a notebook or computer file, is a wise idea. Mastery of the idiom of your discipline is essential. This particularly applies to more complex and difficult concepts, an understanding of which is necessary for your project.

MAKE FULL USE OF THE FLEXIBILITY WHICH THE COMPUTER GIVES TO WRITING

The computer has made the task of drafting and redrafting the thesis much easier. Indeed, screen text may be called 'liquid text'. This is because it can be so quickly changed around, amended, edited, proofread and reorganised. If you are concerned about deleting paragraphs of text in a redraft, the original can be preserved in a separate file. When redrafting is well advanced you might like to print out a hard copy of the text for further correction.

STRIKE AN EFFECTIVE INTERPLAY BETWEEN YOUR WRITING AND ITS DOCUMENTATION

Academic writing is distinctive in that documentation, which reflects the use of reference materials and the results of your investigation, shares an intimate place with writing. It should, therefore, be integrated successfully into the presentation of the thesis to provide tangible evidence of the breadth of your reading, the strength of the documentary defence of your thesis, and your skill in selecting and using your sources. Ensure that you are completely familiar with the referencing system used in your discipline and its detailed implementation.

THE WRITER, THE READER AND THE THESIS

Your thesis may be perceived as a site where you and your reader meet in productive collaboration and mutual understanding. Each will come to the thesis with a set of important questions designed to test its quality, as shown in Table 8.1.

Table 8.1 Differing views of the writer and reader

The writer	Is my thesis clearly stated? Am I convinced of its significance to the field of knowledge? Has this field of knowledge been a continuing point of reference throughout the study?	Have I used my sources and data effectively in the defence of the thesis?	Have I applied my methodology successfully?	Have I used drafting and redrafting to clarify my thoughts and intentions so my writing strongly enhances the project?	Have I effectively integrated data from my investigation and reference material into my thesis?	Have I written a successful thesis?
The thesis						
The reader	Is the thesis or the central issue explored in the study clear and significant to me?	Is the evidence used in the defence of the thesis convincing?	Has the methodology of the thesis been effectively used and presented?	Is the written presentation of the thesis such that it is accessible, interesting and effective?	Does the documentation give me confidence in the integrity of the project?	Is the thesis of such quality that through distinctiveness of perspective and/or originality of approach it adds to the body of knowledge within the field?

Drafting, revising, editing and proofreading

I'm not one of those people who writes endless drafts. I usually tend to write a first draft then a good second draft and then polish that second draft. So I suppose you are talking about two-and-a-half drafts really. However, I approach the task from the point of view of making it as good as I can from the start, and one of the important factors is keeping things in order when you do your research. Being organised in your research helps with writing.

—Tony, a Masters student in Mathematics

Chapter 8 presented general considerations essential to the effective presentation of a thesis. But what of the act of writing itself, as you are confronted with a vacant screen and about to produce the chapters of your thesis? What will productively accelerate the process?

YOU MUST BE READY TO REDRAFT

Redrafting a chapter means rewriting those sections that could be improved so that your argument and its presentation are put as soundly as possible. Almost all writers, including highly experienced ones, redraft.

In the first draft of your thesis you are really finding out what you know. In a sense, you are writing for yourself, so the first draft is experimental. Having got your ideas onto the screen, you then move through the draft making both the substance and the expression as clear as possible to your reader. Drafting allows you to write with the relaxed knowledge that you can later remove any blemishes, large or small, which occur in your writing.

HOW TO WRITE THE FIRST DRAFT

Some writers produce the first draft at one sitting, others over a number of days. The choice depends on the method you find most comfortable and the time available. The plan will be your guide and your paragraphs will reflect the various stages in the plan. At this point you are not concerned with perfection either in content or presentation—the aim is to get your ideas onto screen or paper. If you are using a computer, you can use the 'copy and paste' function to transfer notes and summaries into your draft, there to be restated according to the needs of the chapter.

To avoid a linear 'storytelling' approach to the thesis, you may find it useful to set out the main part of the plan as a series of focal questions to be answered as you write your draft. These might include:

- Why are my results significant?
- How do they provide a strong defence of my thesis?
- Why are the variables in my research significant?
- How do I demonstrate that the methodologies I have used are appropriate for my investigation?
- Are there any philosophical issues that I should raise in relation to my investigation?
- How do I reassure the reader that my results are reliable and valid?
- What were the limitations of the enquiry?
- What proposals are there for further investigation as a result of my research?

Such key questions suggest supporting cues in preparing the chapter.

Most importantly, you will also find that, as you write, other ideas and other ways of tackling problems are likely to come to you. In this sense, the act of writing becomes the act of creation. Certainly you will feel that you are now coming to grips with the chapter.

As you write, be conscious of your aims and how you are responding to them. More technically, be aware of the metacognitive process involved—that is, your goals, the demands of the task, your resources, and the strategies which are going to be used to complete the chapter.

In brief, the successful academic writer develops a series of questions to help with the task:

- Do I need examples to illustrate this point?
- Does this term need to be defined?
- Will this topic sentence be a good premise for this paragraph?
- Is this the time to summon up a citation or quotation to substantiate my point?
- Is this a convincing way to use data from my research? Have I answered objections which might be made to my assertion?
- Am I drawing a defensible inference?

With these questions in mind you will have an objective and appropriate strategy as you write various parts of your text. This active dialogue between you and your writing ensures that you do not write flat, descriptive, unanalytical text.

Why the first draft is so important

Writing the first draft brings your ideas together, enables you to see more clearly the relationships in what you have studied, and provides you with immediate feedback on your approach to the chapter.

The first draft helps you to decide what is possible and what is not: it tests your ideas and pushes you into strong intellectual involvement with the question. Most of all, it tells you what you know and how your presentation can be improved.

HOW TO REDRAFT

Begin with the big picture. Look at the way you have organised your chapter and defended your thesis statement. This stage is called the revision stage and it is essential to the quality of your project. As one expert has put it:

> Skilled writers revise constantly, trying to resolve the tensions between what they want to say, and what the sentences actually record. For many skilled writers, revising is the crux of the writing process. It is the way they shape prose into meaning for an audience, and the way they discover what they want to say, sometimes to their own surprise.
>
> (Yang, 1992)

THE REVISION STAGE

Consider your goals for the chapter and what you were trying to achieve. Look back at the chapter heading and its sub-headings. Now start reading the chapter in full. At this stage you are not interested in correcting spelling and grammatical errors or other comparatively minor aspects. *The overall impact of the chapter, and how comfortably it fits into the total project, is your major concern.* As you read go into 'find mode'. Look for weaknesses in how you put your argument, the structure of the chapter, its interpretative emphases and explanations, and the evidence you have used. Is your theoretical grasp sound and your inferences sustainable? Try to read the chapter as an examiner or specialist in the field would. Mark where the text does not read well, seems unclear, needs rearranging or strengthening. You might like to use symbols such as:

- (?) for lack of clarity
- (c) for points which need to be checked

- (x) for material which might need to be deleted
- (r) for repetitiveness
- (e) for lack of evidence
- (i) for interpretative weakness.

Now you are in a position to move through the text making any necessary corrections through rewriting, deleting or adding material. Your basic aims are to make your meaning as clear as possible and the defence of your thesis, through the chapter, strikingly effective. It may mean that you have to go away and muster additional evidence, reconsider some of your interpretative assertions, redefine some of your key terms, or reorganise the structure of the chapter.

If possible, get someone else to read your text in addition to your supervisor, and discuss it with the reader. Does the reader have any problems with it? You might also like to read it aloud. How does it sound?

What do professional writers say?

Professional writers and educators often refer to the importance of revising what they write:

'All writing that is any good is experimental: that is, it's a way of seeing what is possible.' Penn Edwards

'As you continue writing and rewriting, you begin to see possibilities you hadn't seen before.' Robert Hayden

'I think that one is constantly startled by the things which appear before you on the page when you're writing.' Shirley Hazzard

'Writing and rewriting is a constant search for what one is saying.' John Updike

'Writing has to be an act of discovery ... I write to find out what I am thinking about.' Edward Albee

---

The detection of errors is a positive outcome and their correction is part of the evolutionary development of your thesis. It is interesting that while trial or rehearsal is an integral part of so many activities, its presence in writing (through constructive redrafting) is not so readily acknowledged. Intelligent and reflective revision is essential given its potential for strengthening your work.

EDITING: CREATING 'READER-DIRECTED' TEXT

Editing is about getting your text into good shape for your reader. As mentioned above, when you write a first draft you write for yourself, in order to find out what you know. In revision, you redraft to ensure that your ideas are well organised and convincingly presented. In editing, you redraft wherever necessary to ensure that your thoughts in writing are expressed so clearly that your readers will readily understand what you mean. This is the process of making your text reader-directed.

A reader finds well-edited text easy to read. The reader is not left with the task of trying to infer meaning from poorly written paragraphs and sentences. Unnecessary abstraction and jargon are avoided. When terms specific to the discipline or to particular theorists are used in the text, they are carefully defined. Indeed the writing is so easy to read and understand that the reader starts to know what is coming next. The reader moves into an easy collaboration with the writer as the thesis is read.

The key importance of paragraphs

When you edit, commence with the paragraphs of your chapter. Paragraphs are important because:

- they reflect the structure of your argument
- they control the release of information to your reader
- each paragraph takes the explanation, description or argument of the essay a step further.

Each paragraph—with its premise or topic sentence, supporting sentences (which both explain and defend the thesis), citations and quotes and concluding sentence—reflects the overall argument and is a vital component of its success. It is not surprising that paragraphs have been called the building blocks of a chapter and thesis.

The physical appearance (indented or commencing on a new line) of a paragraph signals to the reader that the argument is moving into another stage in its development. Each paragraph needs to be closely related to the argument of the thesis and the paragraph which precedes and succeeds it. Each paragraph of a chapter is the product of your study, reading, note-taking and reflection on your thesis.

Given their organisational purpose, paragraphs are also likely to be a faithful reflection of your chapter plan. (You may, however, wish to alter your plan after you have completed early drafts of paragraphs.) Paragraphs which are unduly short, which lack internal coherence, or fail to relate to preceding and succeeding paragraphs are examples of wasting the powerful organising and presentation potential of the well-executed paragraph.

Illustrating paragraph structure

An example

The common features of paragraph structure—topic, plus supporting and concluding sentences—can be illustrated in this short paragraph by Timothy Forrest:

> By early adolescence, Piaget believed that children have progressed in their reasoning from a morality of constraint to a morality of co-operation (Dusek 1991). Egocentricism has broken down sufficiently, allowing the young person to understand the intention of a rule—to sustain cooperation and fairness—rather than viewing it in categorical terms. Moral decisions based on principles of reciprocity and fairness thus

> exhibit the highest level of maturity (Durkin 1995). Such decision making is autonomous and allocentric: made, not under duress, but with the good intention of others in mind. (1997, p. 473).

The *topic sentence* or premise (here, the first in the paragraph) is clear from the example. It states Piaget's assertion, an issue essential to Forrest's thesis.

Supporting sentences (the next two sentences) give explanatory support to the topic sentence. As a result of child growth and development and socialisation, moral attributes and capacities are expanding. The supporting sentences also demonstrate the writer's understanding of Piaget's assertion, which can later be used in the analysis of his empirical data.

The *concluding sentence* restates the premise of the morality of cooperation. Note as well that a key term is explained, not merely left to stand, and this explanation becomes part of the concluding sentence.

Transitionals or ties

Be sensitive to words known as transitionals (or ties) which link a sentence with its preceding sentence. Transitionals are usually the first word or words in a succeeding sentence. The presence of transitionals in this extract, from a published research report, is shown in italics:

> *As outlined above,* police studies departments are new to Australian university campuses, and morale was generally reported as high. *This was* the most positive response to this section of the survey. *Indeed the morale* of police educators seems higher than that of other groups in Australian universities (see Mahony, forthcoming; Mahony and Over, 1993). *This result* was also interesting in view of the institutional challenges that confront police educators on campus. Respondents were neutral about the adequacy or otherwise of their

infrastructure and resources 'for the effective delivery of its course and study programs' [16]. We obtained *a similar result* with the institutional regard to police studies [21]. New disciplines and professional programs obviously require time and effort to win strong recognition in universities, and faculty members' research reputation is the most powerful factor for institutional recognition. *Yet the survey suggests* that police studies is finding it difficult to gain adequate funding from outside resources for significant research projects [26]. A majority of respondents viewed teaching and research as the 'first priority' in police studies departments [24] rather than effective teaching [22] or 'effective research' [23]. In this *survey, as noted above,* most respondents described themselves as 'teachers–researchers'.

(Mahony and Prenzler, 1996)

Note that the transitionals or ties help to link a sentence with the one that has gone before, contributing to unity within the paragraph. Indeed, written by itself, a transitional dependent sentence seems incomplete; for example:

This was the most positive response to this section of the survey.

or

Yet the survey suggests that police studies is finding it difficult to gain adequate funding from outside resources for significant research projects [26].

Transitionals make the paragraph flow. They contribute to paragraph coherence, so that it hangs together. But the basic way a paragraph hangs together is through the main idea it introduces and develops. There should also be coherence from paragraph to paragraph as each contributes to the orderly development of your chapter.

The quoted paragraph is also interesting in the way it integrates the results of empirical evidence. The numbered references refer to the number of an item in a survey questionnaire and its results. The paragraph is simply saying that on the evidence of the survey, while the morale of police educators is high, adequate infrastructure and research recognition remain a challenge, particularly as the great majority see themselves as teachers–researchers.

Editing to strengthen your sentences

Having read the sentences in their paragraph setting, you must read each sentence to ensure that it conveys its thought clearly to your reader. Variety in sentence beginnings give added interest to your work. You do not want to bore your reader. And beginnings, like transitionals, help relate a sentence with the one that has gone before. Be careful of sentence length. Unduly long sentences, if they occur repeatedly, make your work more difficult to read. There might be occasions when you split up some of your sentences to improve their readability. This is not to suggest that long sentences be avoided, but that they be mediated with shorter sentences, when appropriate, to assist the general impact of your writing. Ensure that there are no so-called 'talking' or 'non-reader' sentences in your work. These sometimes hang over from a first draft, when your were trying to work out what you wanted to say, and now need to be corrected. The non-reader sentence is often repetitious:

> Within contemporary societies there are many cultures present as a result of immigration. Meaning that in present society there is not only one culture but many.

The second 'sentence' is both unnecessary and incomplete. The expression 'meaning that' should be avoided in a formal context. The sentence could be restated more concisely like this:

As a result of immigration, a multicultural society has been created in many contemporary societies.

Avoid padding

Ensure that padding is edited out of your thesis. Padding occurs when words are used wastefully rather than concisely and effectively, making text more difficult to follow and obscuring the points that you are trying to make. Padding is evident when writers fall into the habit of using unnecessary expressions or when they lack confidence in their topic, and is always the result of poor editing. Compare the following two sentences:

At that time the management group having *given due consideration* to the organisation's work practices were *of the view* that a general meeting of staff *should be held* as an efficient way of reviewing operations and making *appropriate recommendations.*

Management decided that a general meeting of staff could help in determining more efficient work practices.

The first sentence consists of thirty-nine words; the second sentence consists of sixteen words. The unnecessary phrases which clog up the first sentence have been italicised. Verbosity may occur in early drafts as you work out your ideas on paper, or fall into certain stylistic weaknesses. The purpose of editing is to correct these weaknesses before the final draft.

PROOFREADING

Proofreading is concerned with making the penultimate draft free from technical errors in spelling, grammar, usage and punctuation. As indicated earlier, there is no need to closely proofread in earlier drafts because at that stage you are more concerned with the weightier matters of expression of ideas, revision and editing. Nevertheless, the submission of text free of technical errors is a basic requirement for the thesis. You can expect your examiners to pick up the most minor errors, and you should, therefore, ensure that they do not occur in your final draft.

Your computer's spell-check function will help you with spelling errors and 'typos', but it will not correct words that are spelt correctly but are incorrect in the context:

He came dripping *form* the pool.
I will *right* this assignment.

A grammar check may also be helpful, but you have to weigh up its suggestions. Indeed, you must go through your final draft making sure all technical errors are removed so that you can submit a 'fair copy'—that is, a copy of your thesis free of blemishes.

Proofreading your thesis should also ensure that citations are perfectly correct in their attribution and method of presentation. Any weaknesses in this area can expect to draw pointedly adverse comment from assessors.

CONCLUSION

Your goal, of course, is to present a successful thesis. Nothing should be permitted to mar this result. The resubmission of theses for errors which should have been picked up through the revision, editing and proofreading processes is frustrating and disappointing. For this reason, it is wise to allow plenty of time to review your thesis. The journey will have been too long to permit anything to spoil its successful conclusion.

chapter 10

Intellectual property

I had always assumed that I owned the research and outcomes of my thesis. Then I discovered that as my research was a follow-on project from my supervisor's PhD, in his eyes I was only a research assistant fulfilling his need to extend the research for his own ends. After one joint conference paper, my supervisor assumed the results and proceeded to use them without even referring to my work or giving me any credit. There was little that I could do given his high profile in the academic community. I was so naive, I wish I'd understood in the beginning who would own the research outcomes. I guess I thought that I wouldn't do anything particularly significant that needed protecting.

—Benedict, a PhD student in Biochemistry

The term 'intellectual property' refers to various pieces of legislation designed to protect *products of the mind*. Many students begin postgraduate study assuming they will not discover or develop anything of real significance. However, the issue of intellectual property lies at the very heart of postgraduate study. That is, universities are primarily involved in the generation, transmission and consumption of intellectual properties. It is therefore vital that you understand your rights in this area from the beginning.

The degree to which you are involved in generating intellectual property and your ownership of this property needs to be made explicit from the very beginning and discussed with your supervisor. You should negotiate appropriate agreements at the beginning regarding research outcomes with your supervisor or other persons who may have an interest in your research. Each institution should have a policy on the ownership of intellectual property, particularly when generated by students in their course of study or research within the institution. Any understandings between a student and supervisor must be consistent with the institution's policy, which should be made available to postgraduate students at the time of their enrolment.

The Australian Vice-Chancellors' Committee's (AVCC, 1990) code of practice states that if a candidate is involved in work which could result in the generation of intellectual property and/or is funded by a contractual arrangement:

- the candidate should be fully informed by the supervisor, in writing, of any conditions or contract which could either restrict disclosure or affect the extent to which communication with colleagues is possible during the course of the work and its completion
- any delay in publication, e.g. while patent viability is investigated and patent specifications are drawn up and lodged, should be as limited as possible
- the normal maximum delay in publication is twelve months.

The code argues that agreement with regard to intellectual property should be reached between the student and supervisor concerning authorship of publications and acknowledgement of contributions during and after the candidature. The guidelines state that there should be open and mutual recognition of the candidate's and supervisor's contribution on all publication work arising from the project. This code of practice, however, leaves open the question of whether authorship of papers should be shared with the supervisor or whether the candidate should be the sole author of papers. This is a potential point of conflict and needs to be discussed at the beginning of supervision.

Your university will probably have a code of conduct regarding intellectual property. Ask your supervisor or the postgraduate coordinator in your department. Otherwise, there may be a national code for your country or a code for your discipline, e.g. American Psychological Association Guidelines. Ask the relevant postgraduate students' association for further information.

HOW CAN POSTGRADUATE STUDENTS PROTECT THEIR INTELLECTUAL PROPERTY?

The following guidelines are drawn from the Queensland University of Technology's *Copyright Guide*.

Recommendations

The guidelines recommend that students:

- need to be familiar with their country's copyright legislation, knowing what protection their government gives them for creative works
- need to be familiar with the intellectual property policy of their own university
- need to discuss both of the above issues with their supervisor at the onset of their project, and find out if there are any practices within their particular discipline which would disadvantage them in relation to credit for authorship or originality.

If there are policies like the ones described above, students will need to negotiate a mutually satisfactory *written agreement to protect their interests with their supervisor.*

USING OTHER PEOPLE'S WORKS IN RESEARCH DOCUMENTS, CONFERENCE PAPERS AND THESES

The Copyright Act in Australia allows some free use of copyright works, which is referred to as fair dealing. Fair dealing applies only to the following activities:

- research and study
- criticism and review
- news reporting
- reproduction for purposes of judicial proceedings or legal professional advice.

The Act says that you may copy a reasonable portion of a work for any of the above purposes. The Act does not provide any information on the size of a reasonable portion. You must also take several things into account:

- The nature and purpose of the dealing—are you copying for one of the purposes listed above?
- The amount and substantiality of the dealing—how much is being copied and what part of the work—this is a qualitative as well as a quantitative assessment.
- The effect of the dealing on the potential market—will your dealing deprive the copyright owner of revenue?
- The market availability of the item being copied—would it have been easy for you to purchase a new copy of the item being reproduced?

The copyright guidelines cited above suggest that if you can provide appropriate answers for these four areas, then it is likely that the dealing is fair. It should be noted that in no circumstances is the copying of any substantial portion of a work for inclusion in your own publication a fair dealing. If you wish to include copyright material in a work which you plan to publish, permission must be obtained from the copyright owner.

One of the purposes of copyright law is to enable creators to build on the work of others. In academic publishing (conference papers, textbooks, journal articles and the like), quoting from the work of others is a common practice. Here, there can be a fine line between fair dealing and infringement of another author's copyright. If it can be established that you are including portions of other works in your own for the purposes of comment, criticism or review then, provided you have given the author sufficient acknowledgement, the dealing may be fair. If, however, you are using the quoted material merely to convey the same information as the author, for a rival purpose, then that may not be fair dealing, but infringement.

You must also consider the amount of material you are using. Is it a small amount of the other author's work, with substantial comment by yourself (in which case the dealing may be fair) or is it large amounts of the other author's text, with only minimal comment by you (which may render the dealing unfair)?

COPYRIGHT AND PUBLICATION

When you present a manuscript for publication, the publisher will require you to sign an undertaking that you have obtained all relevant permissions in relation to the use of copyrighted works in your own work. If you are uncertain as to whether your use of these works would meet the criteria for fair dealing, you should take steps to obtain permission from the copyright owner to include those portions of their work in your own. Copyright in published works is usually vested in the publisher, and an enquiry to the publisher is the best place to start. Remember that such things as charts, diagrams, tables and maps are complete works, and you will need to request permission to reproduce them.

MATERIAL ON THE INTERNET

When using material which may be found on the Internet, the following guidelines are useful:

- remember that it's all copyright—somebody owns it

- ask for permission to use it; e-mail is quick and cheap
- explain why you want it, where it will be used, and which piece you want
- give the author appropriate credit.

Formats for citing internet material can be found at http://www.cas.usf.edu/english/walker/mla.html—MLA-Style Citations of Electronic Sources, Janice Walker, University of Southern Florida. Remember that putting text on the Internet is a sure way to have it seen by lots of people, so don't plagiarise or you'll get caught.

AUTHORSHIP AND CUSTOMS

Supervisor as first author is a custom which many find completely untenable. It may have been satisfactory in the past, where a doctoral thesis was a collaborative effort, but what of the situation where a student is engaged in groundbreaking research, and is virtually teaching the supervisor as the work unfolds? Joint authorship? Some would suggest, 'No way'. Editor, maybe, but only if the supervisor's contribution merits this level of acknowledgement.

Generally, beware of 'customs' in various disciplines. Find out what they are, if any, before you start. Voice your objections to such practices if you find them uncomfortable. Know the law and the institutional policy. Instances have been found of supervisors taking doctoral work from their students and presenting it as conference papers of their own authorship. This isn't custom—this is theft.

MORAL RIGHTS

The Australian Government will soon be introducing moral rights legislation. It is understood that two rights will be introduced, probably as part of the Copyright Act. These two rights will be the right of attribution and the right of integrity. These rights will remain with the authors of works, they will not be able to be sold or transferred like copyrights.

The right of attribution ensures that the author of a work has the right to be named as the author of that work. Failure to correctly attribute a work will be an infringement of that author's moral rights. The right of integrity will ensure that a work cannot be altered or changed in any way that will impugn the author's honour or reputation.

What the penalties for infringement of these rights will be, or what defences and remedies will be available, is not yet clear, but both of these rights will have many implications for postgraduate students involved in teaching, research and publishing (Queensland University of Technology, 1995).

Case studies

The following case studies illustrate the type of dilemma which may arise from confusion in relation to intellectual property.

Case study

Jake had been working on his PhD in a department of engineering. During the course of his research he collected a large amount of data on agglomeration of nanoscale granular media. During the third year of his doctorate study, his supervisor enquired whether one of his other students, who was undertaking an honours degree, might use part of his data.

Jake had some concerns about this arrangement but, following further discussion with his supervisor, he was assured that he would be first author on any papers which might result from any collaboration between his supervisor and the honours student. The collaboration appeared to work successfully over the twelve-month period and the honours student graduated with his honours degree.

Some months later the honours student, who was now doing his Masters degree, contacted Jake and said that he hoped Jake would not mind but he was planning on presenting a paper at a national conference based on his honours thesis. He also indicated that he assumed it was okay for him to be first author. When Jake contacted their mutual supervisor, the supervisor said in a somewhat offhand way that he trusted the arrangement would work as the student needed the opportunities for conference presentations and publications for his career. This necessitated that the student be first author.

Jake reported being in a dilemma and confused about his rights in the situation. It was clear that his supervisor did not share his concerns. The officer charged with overseeing the administration of intellectual property in the university commented as follows:

This is an extremely difficult issue because it could be argued that Jake's data was a collection of facts and therefore not copyrightable. However, there remains an ethical question about the honours student's behaviour, and Jake would have been wise to have had a written agreement relating to the use of his data at the beginning of this whole saga. This contract might specify the conditions governing attribution of authorship.

Case study

Desley was undertaking a Masters degree in a particular area of the social sciences. She then extended her research to a PhD level. During the course of her research, she collaborated with a supervisor and put together an application for a research grant in both their names. This was submitted to an external funding body. The application was highly recommended but the study was not funded. The university then suggested some changes and offered to fund the project.

Desley believed that the proposed changes would undermine the integrity of the study. As a consequence, she decided to decline the funding and continued with her graduate study in its original format.

Some months later she learned that her supervisor had decided to accept the funding under his own name. He also indicated that he was presenting a paper at a conference based on the research he was supervising. The student was not mentioned as an author of the paper.

The sequence of events caused Desley deep anguish as she was concerned that if she lodged any kind of formal complaint she would jeopardise her relationship with her supervisor. However, she also felt deeply involved in the research project and felt strongly that the proposed study which would be funded was based on the intellectual property which had evolved as a consequence of her Masters degree, and that the integrity of the project had been undermined by the changes which had been made.

An intellectual copyright officer as follows:

Desley's copyright has been infringed by her supervisor. If a face-to-face meeting with the supervisor failed to resolve the issue, her next step would be to consult the Dean of Faculty or, failing that, the Vice-Chancellor or the postgraduate students' association. Desley will have to decide which is most important to her, her professional reputation or her relationship with her supervisor. I would opt for reputation—supervisors are replaceable, especially unconscionable ones who steal the works of another.

Most postgraduate students will be involved in the generation of new material which is their intellectual property. Therefore, you need to have a clear understanding of the issues from the outset. You should discuss this with your supervisor and establish clearly whether they operate under a particular code in this area. Agreement on issues relating to intellectual property should be reached from the very beginning of your research. Be assured, however, that in the majority of instances, students and supervisors work within an affirming and supportive framework with a view to enhancing the knowledge, research skills and career prospects of the student.

chapter 11

Presenting papers and seminars

I really didn't want to do the three presentations that are required but in fact they were invaluable. I strongly recommend that people put a lot of time and effort into presenting papers, because they really do help you to focus. For a start, they give you a timetable; you're forced to do something each year which involves summarising and then communicating your findings. It really helps to crystallise your thoughts.

—Lesley, a PhD student in International Relations

The value of a verbal presentation is that it demonstrates to people that not only have you engaged in a body of research over a number of years, but you can communicate what you are doing, you can argue your position, you can talk about it to people, and you can respond to their queries and criticisms of your work. Particularly if you are going to establish an academic career, there is no point in just being a good writer, squirrelling yourself away in a library or in front of a computer all day; presenting makes you prove that you can communicate your research with other people.

—Julian, a PhD student in Modern Languages

In postgraduate study it is important to participate in academic dialogue. While much of this dialogue may be articulated through writing, it is very likely that you will also be offered the opportunity to make presentations, maybe for other students and academic staff, or at conferences or professional meetings. In the early stages, this participation may involve the presentation of your proposal to the faculty or department; much later you may present a conference paper based on your thesis. In all cases, it is important that you present yourself and your work effectively.

Presentation involves very different skills to those of writing and researching. These skills are easy to develop if you are prepared to practise and take every opportunity to present your ideas. Remember, presenting is like writing in that the more you do the more competent you will become.

PREPARING

Thorough preparation will increase your confidence and thus the effectiveness of your presentation. It is not sufficient simply to write a paper and then read it. You need to think about your audience, the points you want to get across to them and how you will do it. In academic presentations there is sometimes a tendency to 'fog' the audience, that is to present the material in such a way that it appears difficult to comprehend. Presenters who take this approach risk alienating their audience rather than impressing them with their knowledge and competence. Remember, you add value to a presentation by placing your ideas and research findings in a format and language which are meaningful to the audience and allow them to comprehend your work.

Begin preparing by asking yourself the following questions:

- Why am I undertaking this study?
- What are my objectives in making this presentation?
- Who will be in the audience? What is their level of knowledge about the subject?
- How much time is allowed for the presentation? Is there a question time?

- Where will the presentation be held? What facilities are available?
- How will I open and close the presentation?
- How will I organise the body of the presentation?
- What visual aids will I use?
- What questions will I ask the audience?
- What questions will the audience ask me?
- How will I tailor my presentation to the audience?
- What form of prompts (e.g. cards, overheads) will I use?
- Would handouts be useful?
- How will I rehearse?

The key to a good presentation is the establishment of a relationship with the audience. Each of the following questions will help you to develop 'connections' with your audience:

- How do your ideas connect with theirs?
- Why would they be interested in your topic?
- How is the topic relevant to them?

The audience to whom you are presenting and the time available to you will determine the amount of detail which is necessary or possible. Audiences tend to appreciate visual and auditory material in combination, so it is advisable to use some form of visual presentation along with your verbal presentation. If you wish to use an overhead projector, video, computer-aided images or other forms of projection, you need to examine the location early in your preparation to determine the availability and placement of such devices. All such equipment should be trialled—in the location, if possible—before the presentation. Make sure that the whole audience will be able to see the screen or other visuals you will be using. If it is a large room and your voice projection is poor, you may require a microphone.

ORGANISING YOUR MATERIAL

Work out what information you need to cover and in what

order you need to cover it. Figure 11.1 gives an example of a possible structure for organising your presentation.

Draw a diagram of your own reflecting the areas you wish to cover and the relationships between sections. You can use

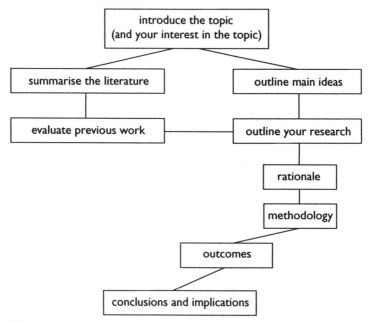

Figure 11.1 The research process

this as an overhead as part of your introduction, indicating to the audience the direction your presentation is going to take.

The laws of primacy and recency in terms of memory suggest that audiences recall best the information delivered at the beginning and end of a presentation. Therefore, you need to focus attention on your introduction and your conclusion. Many professional public speakers use humour at the beginning and end of their speeches for extra impact. If humour comes easily to you, by all means use it, ensuring always that your jokes are in no way discriminatory and will not offend sections of your audience. A funny cartoon drawn on an overhead can be an easy and low-risk way to introduce humour.

It is vital that you understand fully the material which you are presenting. Practise verbalising your ideas to other people. For instance, if you drive to university with friends, tell them about what you are doing; it may make their day more interesting and also give you useful practice in explaining your ideas. There is a tendency for many students undertaking research to avoid trying to explain what they are doing to others not involved in their area because of the difficulties and the often naive questions which follow. Trial runs of your presentation in safe environments such as peer support groups will assist you to iron out difficulties, develop clarity in your explanations and build verbal confidence. They will also give you practice in anticipating and answering questions.

USING PROMPTS

Start to prepare your presentation by writing notes covering all the ideas and concepts which you wish to include. Once you are clear about the order, you need to decide on the prompts you will use. Speakers should never use full written notes. They are a distraction, and it is inappropriate to read notes word for word. After all, you could save the audience time and insult by simply giving them your notes to read for themselves rather than attending your presentation.

Prompts are summaries of the points you want to cover. They can be small cards which you hold in your hand or overheads which you show during your presentation and use to remind yourself of the relevant points. Computer programs such as PowerPoint will provide you with 'lecture notes', as well as producing your overhead transparencies. You can use any other form of summary which is not intrusive to the presentation and allows you to maintain visual contact with the audience.

Each prompt should contain no more than five key points in large print. The points should be in summary form with key words to remind you of further detail you wish to include in your presentation. If you are using overheads, the same principles apply. The advantage of overheads is that the audience is getting visual reinforcement of the information while you are gaining an unobtrusive prompt.

PRESENTING

On the day, choose clothing which is comfortable and appropriate for the occasion. If you feel anxious, find a point on which to focus your eyes at the middle or back of the room. As you begin to feel more comfortable you can look directly at audience members. Keep your head up as much as possible as it aids voice projection and clarity. Aim to keep your body as still as possible so as not to distract from your verbal presentation. We have all been to talks where the speaker paces the room or has annoying repetitive body movements which distract the audience. The eccentric expert may be able to get away with it but the average postgraduate cannot.

The following are some general hints on presentation behaviours:

- At the beginning, get the attention of the audience and explain simply why your topic is of relevance or interest.
- Never hand out printed material at the beginning of the presentation. Audience members will read it or shuffle papers rather than listen to you.
- Make a conscious effort to slow your speech down. Take deep breaths regularly to slow yourself down and to relax.
- At an early stage, ask the audience if they can hear you, and if everyone can see the overheads etc., that you are using.

If you find the whole idea of public speaking difficult, imagine yourself conversing with one person in the audience, with the rest of them simply listening in.

YOUR AUDIENCE

You may think your audience are 'experts' in the field. If so, acknowledge this at the outset of your presentation and enlist their assistance in a positive manner. Even if they are not all experts, constructive analysis and advice from them will be welcome, especially when you are presenting your proposal for the first time and do not yet have expertise in the area. Say something like the following:

I am aware that there are many people in the audience today who are experts in this area. I hope that through your constructive comments and feedback you may be able to assist me with my research.

Often, however, it may only be your perception that the audience are experts, while in reality it is you who are the expert, given that you have spent so much time reading and investigating in this area. Another risk in believing that your audience knows more than they do is that it could tempt you to leave out important explanations of your reasoning process or methodology.

As part of your presentation you may also ask questions of the audience, perhaps in relation to problems you are experiencing, equipment which is difficult to obtain, and so on. For instance, you might ask:

Does anyone have any ideas about how to overcome this problem?
Has anyone had a similar experience?

Novice presenters commonly believe that they must appear as an expert with all the answers, rather than being a person sharing information and ideas with the audience and inviting their cooperation and assistance.

ANTICIPATING AND PREPARING FOR QUESTIONS

Commonly, you may be asked for more explanation of an area, how you intend to overcome a problem, or why you are taking a particular approach. If you have prepared thoroughly, you will be able to handle these questions. Generally, you should anticipate questions and as part of your presentation explain and acknowledge weaknesses rather than waiting for someone else to raise them during question time.

Inevitably, you will also be faced with questions which you haven't anticipated. Always take your time to answer, using verbal techniques to give yourself thinking time. It can also give you time to develop and clarify your response. For instance, you might say:

That's a very good question. I'll need to think a little about that issue before responding.

You can also buy yourself time and clarity by reframing the question and checking with the audience member if that is what they meant:

I think the question you are asking is ... Is that correct?

Always be prepared to admit a lack of knowledge. Then refer the question back to the audience to seek other input:

I'm sorry, I don't have an answer to that. I wonder if anyone else in the audience has any ideas to contribute?

Remember, questions can provide you with a positive opportunity to expand on an area and also to talk about areas you had overlooked in your initial presentation.

What postgraduate students say

What advice would you have for a potential postgraduate student on presenting seminars?

- Be organised and well prepared. Have a trial run at home.
- Know your audience.
- Be prepared, and *know* your stuff.
- *Talk*, don't read.
- Be ready to give an interesting seminar without having to read your notes word for word.
- Anticipate likely comments and questions.

Remember, a thesis is essentially an argument with a beginning, a middle and an end. Giving presentations provides you with an ideal opportunity to articulate the key elements of your argument and also to get feedback from your peers and colleagues on the development of your ideas.

POST-PRESENTATION EVALUATION

The following points will assist you to assess your presentation:

1. Organisation

- Introduction. Was it clear, did it get the audience's attention?
- Body of talk. Were the points clear and did they follow a logical sequence?
- Evidence. Were the supporting evidence and arguments developed?
- Conclusions. Did you round up the presentation well?
- Timing. Did you fit within the time limit and allow time for the most important sections?

2. Delivery

- Did you speak slowly enough?
- Did you have sufficient projection to be heard?
- Did you stand or sit in a comfortable and appropriate manner?

3. Content

- Did you outline your objectives?
- Did you cover the main points?
- Did you explain the main ideas and arguments effectively?

4. Overheads and other visual aids

- Were they clear enough?
- Were they helpful? How would you change them?
- What else could you use?

5. Questions

- Did you handle questions from the audience well?
- How could you have better prepared for them?

- Did you use questions as part of your presentation to involve the audience?

Self-confidence is an important factor in presenting talks and seminars to an audience; the best basis for building this is thorough preparation. If you know the principles—not just the facts—of your subject, prepare your material meticulously, and have a plan worked out for the presentation, you will always be able to give a competent performance.

chapter 12

Assessment and examination of the thesis

I think assessment is a bit hit and miss. It's very much a matter of who chooses your examiners and how they choose them. In my case, I may get an examiner in philosophy and I may get one in politics or they may all be from one field. I think it's just a matter of luck. Half the time you don't know what to expect and you have to rely heavily on your supervisor and hope that they understand the process and have some influence.

—Chuck, a PhD student in Politics/Philosophy

At Oxford everyone has to defend their thesis in a sort of viva situation. I only had to wait six weeks between submitting and defending … It was daunting because I simply didn't know what to expect, whether it would be half an hour, an hour or six hours. But it does make you crystallise your thesis in your mind; you have to be convinced of what you have done. You have to think about what you have written and potential problems … always when you look back on a piece of work you can see flaws after you have been away from it for a few weeks. I think you need to try to go in confidently, but at the same time you need to be prepared for quite severe criticism. I think you should meet that with a good mixture of confidence and acceptance that some of the criticism might be right.

—Joanne, a PhD student in International Relations

The research process is obviously the most vital concern of every candidate, but eventually you will need to face the inevitable assessment process, and it is important from the beginning to know and understand how the assessment process will function. Understanding how the process works will allow you to prepare effectively for it throughout your candidature. There are wide variations between countries and universities, and usually Masters and PhD theses are dealt with differently. In some cases, it is all carried out external to the university, sometimes by overseas examiners with whom you will have no personal contact. In other cases, part of the assessment is carried out within the university through what is known as a thesis/dissertation defence process. Alternatively, a combination of procedures may be used.

Look for written information within your faculty about the assessment process. If this is not available, ask your supervisor to outline the process, making sure they cover the following points:

- Is the thesis assessed internally or externally to the university?
- Who chooses the markers/assessors?
- Can the supervisor or candidate have any input in the selection process?
- Is a thesis defence required? If so, who chooses the panel?
- How do you decide when the thesis is ready to submit?
- What are the possible outcomes (e.g. unconditional/conditional pass)?
- What do the assessment outcomes mean?
- What does an examiner's report usually look like?
- Does a candidate have to comply with examiner's requests for revisions or is there a negotiation process?
- If a thesis is failed, is there anything that a student can do?

These are all questions about the process only, and will allow you to consider what you can do during the development of your thesis to prepare for assessment. If you are able to have some input into the assessors chosen, then you will need to be aware of who the experts in the field are. If you are working in a related field, you will probably be seeking reprints of their published papers and possibly communicating with them about their work if it directly relates to your own. You may meet them at conferences as part of your networking in the academic community, particularly if you are seeking post-doctoral placements. In any case, you will need to know who the experts in the field are and their viewpoints.

It is also vital to understand what assessors are looking for in a thesis, and what criteria they will use in order to assess your thesis. The criteria will vary according to the field of study and the type of investigation involved.

WHAT IS A GOOD THESIS?

A sound thesis will usually have four identifiable components: a proposition, justification, evidence, and proof or conclusion. The thesis should provide a scholarly and critical analysis of the topic, be critical of the author as much as of others, and always point to further work that needs to be done. The thesis must state a position (proposition) and this must be defined clearly and coherently. This position must always be argued or justified (justification) in a way that is fair to what others in the literature might think about the phenomenon with which the thesis is most concerned.

A thesis is not a publication; rather, it is a testimonial in a specific written form, depending on the discipline within which you are working, of the progression of your thinking towards a solution to a particular problem. A doctoral thesis should make a substantial contribution to the area of the discipline in which the thesis is written, and contain a significant amount of publishable material. A Masters thesis, while of less depth and breadth than a doctoral thesis, should often contain sufficient material to publish at least one journal article.

Other criteria which students should attend to in their preparation for assessment are outlined by Sheehan (1994).

Quality vs quantity

Students should avoid thinking that the sheer volume of work produced will necessarily impress examiners. Quality of scholarship is what is always primary, provided the previously mentioned criteria are met.

Format

Format and presentation are important. Even though the research work can be criticised methodologically, no examiner should be led to assume that these result from an untidy mind because there are blemishes in presentation. A model of clarity and exposition sets the stage for an uncritical examiner. If the research can't be perfect, at least the format can.

Critical tone

A thesis should primarily demonstrate evidence of analytical ability. Whatever the area of the thesis or its approach to the discipline, there should be evidence that the student appreciates the possible limitations of what they have done.

Impartiality

Personal references should be avoided, but you should always be careful to present alternative viewpoints to the theory that is being preferred so that the assessor can know that other options were considered.

Style

The best theses are those that are written in such a way so as to enthuse the reader about the phenomena being investigated and the candidate's commitment to research. Rewriting is often necessary to achieve this goal and requires intensive liaison with the supervisor.

CRITERIA FOR ASSESSMENT

The following questions will give you some guidance for assessing your own thesis for its readiness for the assessment process.

Evidence of an original investigation or the testing of ideas

- Was the aim of the research clearly described?
- Were the hypotheses to be tested, questions to be answered or methods to be developed clearly stated?
- Was the relationship between the current and previous research in related topic areas defined, with similarities and differences stressed?
- Are the nature and extent of the original contribution clear?

Competence in independent work or experimentation

- Was the methodology employed appropriate? Was its use justified and was the way it was applied adequately described?
- Were variables which might influence the study recognised and either controlled in the research design or properly measured?
- Were valid and reliable instruments used to collect the data?
- Was there evidence of care and accuracy in recording and summarising the data?
- Is evidence displayed of knowledge of, and the ability to use, all relevant data sources?
- Were the limitations inherent in the study recognised and stated?
- Were the conclusions reached justifiable in the light of the data and the way they were analysed?

An understanding of appropriate techniques

- Given the facilities available, did it seem that the best possible techniques were employed to gather and analyse data?
- Was full justification given for the use of the techniques selected and were they adequately described?

- Were the techniques properly related to the stated aims of the research?

Ability to make critical use of published work and source materials

- Was the literature referenced pertinent to the research?
- To what extent could general reference to the literature be criticised on the grounds of insufficiency or excessiveness?
- Was evidence presented of skills in searching the literature?
- Was due credit given to previous work for ideas and techniques used by the author?
- Is evidence displayed of the ability to identify key items in the literature and to compare, contrast and critically review them?

Appreciation of the relationship of the special theme to the wider field of knowledge (for PhD theses only)

- Was the relationship between the current and previous research in related topic areas defined, with similarities and differences stressed?
- Was literature in related disciplines reviewed?
- Was an attempt made to present previous work within an overall conceptual framework and in a systematic way?

Worthy, in part, of publication

- Was the organisation of the report logical and was the style attractive?
- With appropriate extraction and editing could the basis of articles or a book be identified?

Originality as shown by the topic researched or the methodology employed (for PhD theses only)

- To what extent was the topic selected original?
- Was there evidence of innovation in research methodology compared with previous practice in the field?

Distinct contribution to knowledge

- What new material was reported?
- To what extent would the new material be perceived as a valuable addition to a field of knowledge?
- To what extent do the conclusions overturn or challenge previous beliefs?
- Were the findings compared with the findings of any similar studies?
- Was the new contribution clearly delimited and prospects for further work identified?
- To what extent does the work open up whole new areas for future research?

(Howard and Sharp, 1983, pp. 207–208)

CHOICE OF EXAMINERS

Policies in relation to students having a say as to who their examiners will be varies from supervisor to supervisor, institution to institution and country to country. It is important that you ascertain how examiners are chosen in your institution and in your discipline. If you are able to exercise choice as to who your examiners will be, it is wise to go for the very best experts in the field who are highly knowledgeable on the topic. Such people not only have an excellent grasp of the area but also have the breadth to appreciate that a thesis may not be perfect but still makes a valid contribution to knowledge. It is important that you demonstrate your familiarity with the work of the acknowledged experts in your field, as they may end up marking your thesis regardless of whether you have a choice in the selection of markers or not.

THESIS OR DISSERTATION DEFENCE

Thesis or dissertation defence is a practice which is carried out in some universities as an adjunct to external assessment of the thesis, and in others is the principal manner in which the thesis or dissertation is assessed. If you have had to defend your thesis proposal in the early stages to a forum in your faculty or department, then you will have some idea of how the process may occur. However, the thesis defence is usually a very different process and obviously carries with it much greater significance in terms of outcomes.

Depending on the department or faculty, the thesis or dissertation defence may involve a meeting between the candidate and three or more academic staff, who may be members of your department or members of other departments with related and relevant interests, judged capable of assessing the thesis. The panel structure and process will vary greatly, so it is important if this is part of your assessment process to ask your supervisor or head of department for details.

Regardless of how you expect the process to happen, you need to prepare thoroughly, expecting challenging questions. Unlike the thesis proposal stage, it will not be acceptable not to know or be unable to explain why you have done what you have done.

You need to prepare overall in three major ways:

- Develop a complete and verbally fluent account of the substance of the thesis.
- Be ready to present the thesis in a persuasive form for an audience.
- Ensure you have the emotional and personal readiness to manage and deal with the situation.

As this is an exam, it is necessary to prepare for it verbally. You need to practise verbalising your thesis or telling your story. You can do this by using a tape-recorder or by practising with your peer support group as described in chapter 7. Basically, you need to know your thesis inside out and be able to discuss without prompting aspects which assessors may raise and desire further clarification of. You also must anticipate areas of potential weakness or areas which particular assessors with expertise will pick on. Always anticipate the worst in terms of questions and criticisms and prepare for them. If you have kept a journal throughout the process and recorded the rationale for decisions, it may be useful at this point to review it. Any opportunity to tell, discuss or debate your thesis should be taken and used as an opportunity to practise for the thesis defence. Encourage others to challenge you in order to build your defence.

When preparing to present your thesis in a persuasive form to the panel, remember that some panel members may not have had a chance to read your thesis as a whole. They may rely heavily on your abstract together with a quick read of the thesis. This means that your abstract is vital to the first impression that these members receive. Make sure that your abstract gives a concise and precise overview of your thesis, ensuring the problem is stated clearly, with emphasis on the contribution your research has made through the methodology used and clearly described outcomes and ongoing implications.

In order to prepare yourself emotionally for the thesis defence it is important to understand potential processes which may take place as the panel works to assess your thesis. You might think of it as being similar to a job interview which is carried out by a panel. There are always personal interests and investments held by panel members and you may suffer as a result of their need to fulfil these interests. There is likely to be a core of three people who could be regarded as central to the process and the others may be a little more external to it. It is important to prepare for both groups, anticipating that the less central members will have special interests and may pick on specific parts of the thesis which they regard as their area of expertise. They may have some interest in showing their area of expertise to others on the panel. This may mean that you are subjected to difficult questions in that area or that a discussion between members of the panel may develop about the area. Obviously, the nature of the process depends a lot on the individuals involved.

Role-playing the situation, with peers playing the parts of assessors asking questions, is the most effective and realistic way of preparing emotionally for the situation. Make sure your peers play devil's advocate by asking provocative and difficult questions. If you know who will be on your panel of assessors for the thesis defence, other students may role-play particular individuals whose style they know.

AND FINALLY …

Remember that it is quite normal human behaviour for someone who has been asked to assess a thesis or any other document to feel that they have not 'done their job' unless they find something wrong with it which needs correcting. It could be something as minor as a comma here or there, or something more major which is associated with their area of expertise and which they may wish to demonstrate and reaffirm to themselves and others. Therefore, it is important to enter any assessment process at this level realising that a conditional pass subject to minor or major revisions is a common outcome. Entering the process with a black and white, pass or fail mentality is likely to induce increased stress and thus potentially impair your performance. It is common for students to feel at this stage that they have had it and can't do any more, and therefore want the thesis to be unconditionally passed—in most systems an unlikely outcome.

If you are conditionally passed with revisions, this is regarded as a success and should be celebrated as such. Revisions should be tackled as quickly as possible, after you have gained a clear understanding of what is required by the assessor. Usually this process involves continuing close liaison with your supervisor to determine the exact nature of the modifications required. At times, there are negotiations between assessors requesting different modifications, and this process should be overseen by your supervisor.

chapter 13

Careering into the future

I guess I couldn't have got my present position as a lecturer without a PhD, but I'd say the research experience and the learning process you go through doing a postgraduate degree is the most valuable experience of all. You simply learn a tremendous amount and I've found the knowledge and skills I have gained to be most valuable in my teaching at the moment. So never mind the piece of paper, never mind the actual qualification, just the amount of knowledge that you accrue and the kinds of techniques and skills you acquire will be of great benefit.

—Ali, a PhD graduate in Linguistics

Initially, I thought that having a PhD would be the be-all and end-all, then I got near the end and realised what a let down it was. Eventually, I could see that I'd gained a lot by undertaking postgraduate study—lots of new computer skills and research skills and basically I realised that I could write, so I started focussing on the skills I had acquired rather than the qualification. I then used these skills to start up my own consultancy business which has been highly successful.

—Mark, a PhD graduate in Information Technology

Increasingly graduates are being encouraged to undertake postgraduate studies, and larger numbers than ever before are choosing this option. Why? What benefits might the graduate obtain from undertaking such studies, in particular those that require the completion of a major research project? How might a research degree equip one for the future?

The one thing of which we can be sure of today is change, and the change that is occurring is happening at an even faster rate than ever before. The knowledge base of the world is increasing exponentially. The influence of technology and its effect upon communication has been at the forefront of this change, and it is increasingly difficult to keep up, even in one's own area of specialisation, and even with access to excellent resource materials, including the information superhighway. What type of person is going to cope in the world of tomorrow? Surely those with the largest knowledge base will be best equipped?

Postgraduates will be well equipped to cope with the challenges of the future; however, this will not necessarily be as a consequence of a superior knowledge base, although this may certainly be true within their specialist area, i.e. the field in which they have completed their research. Rather, they are likely to succeed because of the skills that they have either acquired or enhanced through the completion of their research.

Jennifer James, an international authority on change, in a keynote address to the Australian Association of Careers Counsellors annual conference in 1997 stated that 'the knowledge worker will rule the world', that 'we have to prepare for a brains, technology and services world' and that 'new forms of intelligence are required'. These 'new forms of intelligence' include: information retrieval skills; strategic thinking and problem-solving abilities; the ability to organise and synthesise; reflective analytical skills; intuitive skills; communication skills; creative and innovative thinking; and relationship and teamwork ability. Each of these skills, or new forms of intelligence, is likely to be enhanced by the successful undertaking of postgraduate studies, in particular those studies that require the completion of an independent research project.

New forms of intelligence are required

As it is very difficult to keep up to date with all that is happening, even in one's own area of knowledge, the capacity to be able to retrieve information is essential. In completing a major research project, which is either expanding on some existing knowledge or discovering some completely new concepts, one's information retrieval skills will surely be enhanced while undertaking a review of related previous research undertaken and published.

While a careful examination of previous research provides an essential base of knowledge upon which to build a research project, more importantly, perhaps, it enhances one's information retrieval skills. A capacity for innovative, creative and intuitive thought, accompanied by excellent problem-solving skills, are likely to be required for the successful completion of any research project, since a research project that goes strictly to plan and time is likely to be the exception rather than the norm.

Furthermore, the capacity to build a positive working relationship with one's supervisor and other research colleagues will require effective communication, interpersonal relationships and teamwork.

Thus, each of the 'new forms of intelligence' described are also likely to be developed or enhanced while undertaking a major research project. Through the acquisition or enhancement of each of these major skills the postgraduate is likely to enhance their capacity for further successful research and employment.

Similarly, as the postgraduate develops and enhances these skills, their sense of personal wellbeing and growth will be actualised and their capacity for further success—be it in research or employment—will be heightened.

What about opportunities in the world of work? One of our greatest challenges is to successfully manage one's career in the ever-changing world of work.

What has been the employment outcome for postgraduates, especially those who have completed a PhD or Masters by research degree?

Recent surveys, completed by organisations responsible for charting the employment outcomes of graduate and postgraduate students in countries such as the United States, United Kingdom and Australia, have shown that the majority of postgraduates who were available for employment have been in the workforce within a short time of graduation. Results of recent surveys of Australian postgraduate students showed that 92.9 per cent of those who had completed a PhD and 88.4 per cent of those who had completed a Masters degree by research were in employment (Graduate Careers Council of Australia, 1995). It is also worth noting that 5.7 per cent of those who had completed a postgraduate qualification were seeking employment at the time of the survey by comparison with 9.1 per cent of graduates. 'While obtaining paid employment is influenced by a number of factors other than educational attainment, the possession of a postgraduate qualification would seem to make a positive contribution' (Graduate Careers Council of Australia, 1995).

WHERE HAVE POSTGRADUATES MOST RECENTLY FOUND THEIR EMPLOYMENT?

While it is difficult to generalise regarding the employment outcomes across even the major industrialised nations, the majority of persons who complete postgraduate studies are likely to be found working within one of two employment sectors, the education or public sector. That is, they are likely to be working in some form of teaching and/or research position within an academic institution or working directly for a government organisation, or an organisation funded by government. The proportion of postgraduate students who have gained initial employment on immediate completion of their studies within the private sector has been much smaller.

An example of this distribution within the Australian context is seen in Table 13.1 which shows the sectors in which those who have completed a PhD or a Masters degree by research and who were available for employment have gained employment.

As can be seen, in recent times the largest proportion of postgraduates with a PhD could be found working in the education sector of the workforce. Indeed, 56 per cent of all PhD graduates who responded to the 1995 *Postgraduate*

Table 13.1 Employment distribution of research graduates

| PhD graduates | Area of employment% | | | |
	Govt	Private	Education	Other
Male/Female	26	16	56	2
Male	27	17	54	2
Female	24	15	58	3
Masters by research graduates				
Male/Female	33	28	36	3
Male	31	34	31	3
Female	33	20	42	3

Destination Survey stating that they were in full-time employment indicated that they were employed in the education sector. This compared with 26 per cent in the government sector and 16 per cent in the private sector. When considering the destination outcomes of postgraduates with a Masters degree by research, it was found that 36 per cent were in the education sector, 33 per cent were in the government sector and 28 per cent were in the private sector.

WHAT DOES THE FUTURE HOLD?

The winds of change affecting the labour market include: organisational restructuring that is not restricted to any single area of the workforce; a demand for increasing levels of competence, with the accompanying pressure to keep up to date and expand one's skill level; and an ability to make best use of the available technology. Associated with the organisational restructuring mentioned above is the disappearance of traditional career structures, career paths and the concept of a job for life.

The number of tenured staff within the higher education sector is decreasing and, with the trend towards the delivery of educational instruction through multimedia technologies and the associated introduction of the 'virtual university', this is likely to be a continuing trend. It is recognised, however, that opportunities for employment within the education sector will continue to remain stable and, in 'developing' countries, continue to grow for some time. Areas of employment such as the public service, which in the past seemed to offer the most security of tenure, have also been significantly affected, with staff reductions and redundancies.

These changes are likely to affect the career choices of postgraduates who, as noted above, have traditionally obtained employment in the education and government sectors, areas that are not isolated from the winds of change sweeping the labour markets of highly industrialised countries. Indeed, the trends that are currently being observed in the United States indicate that increasing numbers of postgraduates, in particular PhD students, are going into business and industry rather than academe and the federal government.

In place of the traditional career choice of a position offering security of tenure, increasing numbers of people will be employed to complete various projects on a short-term contract basis. Others are likely to create their own positions and work for themselves rather than become an employee.

While it has been predicted that the biggest growth in jobs will be for graduates and trained persons, the demand is unlikely to be evenly spread. Some graduates will continue to be in greater demand and employers will be looking for those with a broad base of skills, as noted earlier with reference to the 'new intelligences', not merely specialist skills.

Service industries are likely to account for most of the new jobs, with business, health and education services accounting for 70 per cent of the growth within the services sector (see Figure 13.1). Furthermore, employment in the professional speciality occupations is projected to account for most job growth. These jobs require high educational attainment and offer high earnings. Significant numbers of future graduates and postgraduates will likely find themselves working in positions that do not even currently exist at present. Therefore, an open mind regarding employment possibilities is essential.

It has been projected that the jobs requiring the most education and training will grow faster than those jobs with lower educational and training requirements (see Figure 13.2).

As noted in these figures, occupations which require a Bachelors degree or above will average 23 per cent growth, almost double the 12 per cent growth projected for occupations that require less education and training.

While the postgraduate may be well equipped for the work-force in terms of the skills, competencies, personal qualities and qualifications they possess, without previous work experience their opportunities may well be limited. While the postgraduate who has undertaken research studies may well have experience in research that will be of great advantage for positions requiring

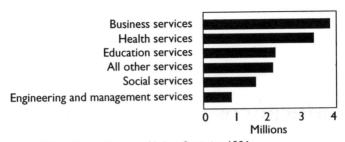

Reference: United States Bureau of Labor Statistics, 1996

Figure 13.1 Projected employment change in service industries, 1994–2005

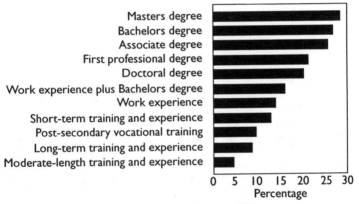

Reference: United States Bureau of Labor Statistics, 1996

Figure 13.2 Projected percentage growth in employment by level of education and training, 1994–2005

such experience, it will be to the postgraduate's advantage to gain additional experience in the workforce, either prior to or in conjunction with their postgraduate studies.

When considering entry to the workforce, the postgraduate, like others, is well advised to consider a broad range of work opportunities in keeping with their interests and work-related values. It is important to generate opportunities before making decisions.

All in all, the postgraduate is well placed in today's changing world.

References

Australian Vice-Chancellors' Committee 1990, *Code of Practice for Maintaining and Monitoring Academic Quality and Standards in Higher Degrees*. Canberra: Australian Vice-Chancellors' Committee.

Bureau of Labor Statistics 1996, US Department of Labor, Washington DC.

Commonwealth Tertiary Education Commission 1986, *Review of Efficiency and Effectiveness in Higher Education*. Canberra: Australian Government Publishing Service.

Covey, S.R. 1990, *The 7 Habits of Highly Effective People*. Melbourne: Business Library.

Cullen, D.J., Pearson, M., Saha, L.J. and Spear, R.H. 1994, *Establishing Effective PhD Supervision*. Canberra: Australian Government Publishing Service.

Durkin, K. 1995, *Developmental Social Psychology from Infancy to Old Age*. Oxford: Blackwell Publishers.

Dusek, J. 1991, *Adolescent Development Behaviour*. 2nd edition. Englewood Cliffs, New Jersey: Prentice Hall.

Forrest, T. 1997, An ethnomethodological perspective upon citizenship education. Unpublished paper, Griffith University, Brisbane.

Graduate Careers Council of Australia 1995, *Postgraduate Destination Survey*.

Handy, C. 1989, *The Age of Unreason*. London: Arrow Books.

Howard, K. and Sharp, J.A. 1983, *The Management of a Student Research Project*. Gower: Aldershot Hants.

Madsen, D. 1983, *Successful Dissertations and Theses*. San Francisco: Jossey-Bass.

Mahony, D. 1997, *Writing for Meaning*. Brisbane, Griffith University.

Mahony, D. and Over, R. 1993, 'Teacher education in Australian universities in a period of change: Predictions and preferences for the year 2000'. *Higher Education* 26:147–165.

Mahony, D. and Prenzler, T. 1996, 'Police studies, the university and the police service: An Australian study'. *Journal of Criminal Justice Administration* 7, 2:283–304.

Moses, I. 1985, *Supervising Postgraduates HERDSA Green Guide No. 3*. Kensington: Higher Education Research and Development Society of Australasia.

Moses, I. 1992, *Research Training and Supervision*. Proceedings of the Australian Research Council and Australian Vice-Chancellors' Committee Conference on Research and Training and Supervision. Canberra: Australian Vice-Chancellors' Committee and Australian Research Committee.

Parry, S. and Hayden, M. 1994, *Supervising Higher Degree Research Students*. Canberra: Australian Government Publishing Service.

Phillips, E.M. and Pugh, D.S. 1994, *How to Get a PhD*. 2nd edition. Buckingham, England: Open University Press.

Powles, M. 1988, *Know Your PhD Students and How to Help Them*. Melbourne: Centre for the Study of Higher Education, University of Melbourne.

Queensland University of Technology 1995, *Copyright Guide*. Queensland University of Technology, Brisbane.

Ryan, Y. and Whittle, J. 1996, 'Principles of adult learning in postgraduate education.' in O. Zubert-Skerrit *Frameworks for Postgraduate Education*. Lismore: Southern Cross University Press, pp. 164–177.

Sheehan, P. 1994, 'From thesis writing to research application: Learning the research culture' in O. Zubert-Skerritt and Y. Ryan (eds) *Quality in Postgraduate Education*. London: Kogan Page, pp. 14–23.

Sternberg, D. 1981, *How to Complete & Survive a Doctoral Dissertation*. New York: St. Martins Press.

Whittle, J. 1992, 'Research culture, supervision practices and postgraduate performance' in O. Zubert-Skerritt and N. Knight (eds) *Starting Research—Supervision and Training*. Brisbane: University of Queensland Press.

Yang, Y. 1992, 'Supporting writing with an undo mechanism' in P. O'Brien-Holt and N. Williams (eds) *Computers and Writing, State of the Art*. London: Kluwer.

Further reading

Ballard, B. and Clanchy, J. 1997, *Teaching International Students: A Brief Guide for Lecturers and Supervisors*. Deakin, ACT: IDP Education Australia.

Cryer, P. 1996, *The Research Student's Guide to Success*. Buckingham, England and Philadelphia: Open University Press.

Elphinstone, L. 1995, *Manual for Supervisors of Postgraduate Students*. Educational Quality Assurance, Research and Development, RMIT, Melbourne.

Lipson, A. and Perkins, D.N. 1990, *BLOCK: The New Psychology of Counterintentional Behavior in Everyday Life*. New York: Lyle Stuart.

Zubert-Skerritt, O. 1996, *Frameworks for Postgraduate Education*. Lismore: Southern Cross University Press.

Index